SUCCESSFUL MARKETING
STRATEGIES
IN AMERICAN INDUSTRY

To my parents
ROY AND JESSIE UDELL
on their
Golden Wedding Anniversary

Successful Marketing Strategies
in American Industry

by

JON G. UDELL
Professor of Business
Graduate School of Business Administration
The University of Wisconsin–Madison

Published by Mimir Publishers Inc.
Madison, Wisconsin

Printed in the U.S.A. by
Worzalla Publishing Company
Stevens Point, Wisconsin

FOREWORD

The reader should find this book of empirical interest because it presents information on the marketing strategies for hundreds of successful products. However, a more important objective is to present a realistic and useful conceptual foundation for determining an appropriate nonprice competitive strategy in today's economic environment.

Two studies, conducted some years apart, provide the empirical foundation for testing a suggested marketing decision model. While this model is not so precise that it will enable the executive to easily and accurately develop an optimum marketing strategy, it does provide a conceptual approach for allocating the firm's resources among the nonprice elements of the marketing mix. For the economist, it suggests a new theoretical foundation for explaining the nonprice competitive behavior of the business firm. Hopefully, this book will be of value to both the pragmatic business executive and the theoretician.

The author is indebted to the over 600 business executives who participated in two studies and generously shared information concerning the marketing strategies for their most successful products. Also greatly appreciated is the financial support of the Graduate School of Business of The University of Wisconsin and the Graduate School of Business and Public Administration of Cornell University.

While several colleagues were of help, the assistance of Professor J. Howard Westing of The University of Wisconsin, Professor Evan Anderson of Tulane University, and Mr. Anthony Hourihan of Harvard University is especially appreciated. A note of thanks is also due to Mrs. Jean Robertson, Miss Ardis Hoffmann, and Mrs. Gay Leslie, who provided excellent secretarial and editing services.

J. G. U.

Madison, Wisconsin
June, 1972

This book has been set in 11 point Baskerville type face leaded one point and printed on 70 lb. white Ibsen Eggshell book paper. The cloth cover is of the highest grade Roxite Library Buckram illustrated with gold leaf impression.

INTRODUCTION

With advancing technology and increasing productivity, the future growth of the economy will depend considerably on the efficiency and effectiveness of marketing programs. Despite the huge size and rising costs of these programs, little research effort has been devoted to measuring and explaining the relative importance of various marketing activities. One unfortunate consequence of this lack of research is a dearth of information, concepts, and theories to guide management decision making.

Especially needed is a pragmatic conceptual explanation of the role of nonprice competitive strategy in the behavior of the business firm. Without better information and an appropriate conceptual framework for analysis and decision making, future progress in improving the efficiency and effectiveness of marketing programs is unlikely.

Unfortunately, neither economists nor business theorists have developed a theory of competitive or marketing behavior which is appropriate in the dynamic business environment of the 1970s. More specifically, they have not adequately coped with the nonprice elements of competitive strategy or the oligopolistic market structure of modern industry. Therefore, the primary objective of this book is to provide a useful decision model for explaining and determining the nonprice competitive strategy of the business firm in an oligopolistic environment.

The effort to develop the conceptual foundation included:

1. The development of a decision model of nonprice competitive strategy which includes two basic hypotheses—one concerned with the product facet of marketing strategy, the other with marketing communications and other sales efforts.

2. Two studies of the marketing strategies for successful products. The results of these studies provide the empirical evidence necessary to evaluate the proposed model.

The book rests primarily on the foundation provided by the latter of the studies and includes an analysis of the marketing strategies for 485 successful products. Considerable effort has been devoted to presenting information on each of the specific industries included in the research. Especially well represented

are the industrial goods industries such as aerospace and defense, capital equipment, prefabricated parts and materials, and industrial chemicals.

Chapter I presents an executive summary of the total book. The second chapter discusses the role of science in business and the need for a realistic theoretical foundation for business decision making. Also included is a discussion of the theoretical attempts that have been made to explain business behavior in the marketplace. Chapter III examines the dynamic environment of industry and reveals how this environment has changed dramatically over the years.

Chapter IV is concerned with the perceived importance of the elements of marketing strategy. Both the major facets— price, product, sales effort and distribution— and the specific elements of those facets are included in the presentation. The data are classified according to three major types of industries, industrial goods, consumer durables, and consumer nondurable goods.

In Chapter V, a decision model for nonprice strategy is presented. Also provided is an empirical evaluation of that model.

Chapter VI is devoted to the marketing strategies of various industrial goods industries. In addition, the information offers a further validation of the decision model. The marketing strategies of various consumer goods industries are the subject of Chapter VII.

The eighth chapter is concerned with the pricing problem of modern industry and the role that various pricing policies play in the strategies of 13 different industries. Chapter IX is devoted to the possible roles of sales volume and share of market in explaining differences in competitive strategies. Also included is information on the marketing costs of various U.S. industries.

The concluding chapter suggests how the product-market decision model might be used by the business executive in evaluating and improving his marketing strategy.

Also included is an appendix which provides a pedagogical approach to visualizing and managing the competitive strategy of the firm. For those who are not versed in economics, the Appendix and certain parts of Chapter II may be somewhat difficult to follow. However, this should not interfere with the reader's ability to grasp the message of this book.

CONTENTS

CHAPTER I

EXECUTIVE SUMMARY

Product development, product service, marketing communication and other nonprice facets of competitive strategy play a prominent role in the marketing behavior of modern industry. The importance of these nonprice facets has increased with the ascent of the buyers' market and the growth of oligopolistic industries.

An oligopolistic industry has only a few competitors. As a consequence, the actions of one rival often have a profound effect on all other companies in the industry. For example, the reduction of price by one firm may force all companies in the industry to reduce their prices, and the ultimate result may be a price war. This interdependence among oligopolists favors the development of real and fancied product differences which usually are more difficult to match than a change in price. Equally important, successful product differentiation gives a company some degree of pricing freedom and market share protection.

Consumers also desire product differentiation. Individual needs and tastes vary widely; product differentiation provides variety and enables consumers (industrial and ultimate consumers) to better satisfy their individual needs and desires.

The growth of affluence and discretionary income has also affected the nature and scope of competitive strategy. Discretionary dollars give the consumer economic bargaining power. By definition, these dollars do not have to be spent on the necessities of life; consequently the consumer is free to save or to spend them on a vast variety of product alternatives. This, coupled with an advanced technology which often brings fairly unlike products into direct competition (note the variety of diverse building materials which are direct rivals), has a pro-

found influence on competition and marketing strategy.

As a consequence of the changes that have occurred, it is no longer realistic to limit the theory of competitive behavior to pricing, nor is it possible to explain competitive behavior in terms of the market structure of a specific industry. Not only is competition intra- and inter-industry in scope, market structure is incapable of explaining or prescribing an optimum nonprice competitive strategy.

With the support of the Graduate School of Business of The University of Wisconsin and the Graduate School of Business and Public Administration of Cornell University, the author has initiated a program to study the marketing strategies of successful U. S. companies and to develop a decision model for nonprice competitive strategy.

Nonprice Strategy Most Important

Established economic doctrine perceives pricing as the major facet of business behavior in the marketplace. However, business management vigorously disagrees.

Financial information was used to select a sample of profitable and expanding U.S. manufacturing companies. In addition, each participating executive was asked to select a product which was successful in terms of its contribution to the sales and profits of the company. Underlying this approach is the heroic assumption that the successful products of profitable and expanding companies would have marketing programs which approach an optimal strategy.

The executives were asked to estimate the relative importance of the competitive activities used in marketing the selected product. In each question, they allocated 100 points among the activities according to the estimated contribution of each to the success of the product. For example, the total marketing program was divided into four major facets:

> *Product Effort*—Includes product planning, product research and development, product testing, and the services accompanying the product.

> *Sales Effort*—Includes sales management and personal selling, advertising, and other promotional programs.

[2]

Distribution—Includes the selection, development, and evaluation of distribution channels, transportation, and inventory control.

Pricing Strategy—Includes price determination, pricing policies, and pricing strategies.

Prior to allocating 100 points among the four major facets of marketing strategy, the executives evaluated the relative importance of the various activities which constitute each facet. For example, product effort is composed of technical research and development, presale service, post-sale service, marketing research relating to the development of products and, for some manufacturers, style R & D. The evaluation of the specific activities preceded the overall evaluation of the major facets in order to insure that respondents had a common understanding of what was included in each of the four major components of the marketing mix.

As shown in Figure I-1, *the average respondent allocated only 18 percent of 100 points to the pricing facet of competitive strategy.* Product effort activities were perceived to be of considerably greater importance, receiving 28 percent of the total strategy points.

Sales effort, or marketing communication, was perceived to be of greatest importance in the success of most products. On the average, 41 points were allocated to advertising, sales, and other promotional activities. This dimension of the marketing mix is even more important than the 41 points imply because the distribution facet included the selection and development of the channel of distribution. To a considerable extent, these are sales effort activities because when any channel other than producer-consumer is used, the manufacturer is shifting part of its sales effort responsibilities to the middlemen involved. Of the 12 points allocated to distribution, over one-half were for the determination, selection, and development of channels of distribution. Therefore, the average respondent attributed almost 50 percent of his product's success to the sales effort activities of competitive strategy.

All types of producers—industrial, consumer durable, and consumer nondurable—selected sales efforts as most important. The

only respondents who ranked product efforts over sales efforts were producers of aerospace and defense equipment for the government. *Business evidently considers the creation of markets more important than the creation of products.* Inasmuch as the creation of products is also considered highly important, the emphasis on sales efforts may be appropriate. As Joseph Schumpeter, the "father" of innovation theory pointed out, invention alone does not foster economic growth or yield profits. It is through the implementation of an invention that progress and profits are achieved. For example, an unpromoted and unmarketed cure for cancer would not contribute to the society's well-being. Likewise, a manufacturer cannot recover its R & D and production costs unless the product is successfully promoted and sold.

Toward A Theory Of Marketing Strategy

Economists have developed a few models which recognize the nonprice factors of competitive strategy. These models usually suggest that the dominant factor in both price and nonprice strategy is the market structure of the industry (for example, competitive, oligopolistic, or monopolistic) or the conditions of entry into the industry. However, one would not expect the marketing strategy of an electronic computer manufacturer to be similar to that of a cosmetic producer if the structures of their industries happened to be similar. Similar competitive conditions might induce like pricing practices, as economic theory suggests, but the companies' nonprice competitive strategies should vary according to the nature of the firms' products and the characteristics of the relevant consumers (and perhaps numerous other variables).

The author's hypothesis is that *the competitive strategy, and consequently the importance of the various marketing activities, will vary according to the nature of the product and its market.* The latter factor, the market—its desires, behavior, and characteristics—is most important. More specifically, it is hypothesized that the consumers' knowledge concerning the product, the effort they expend in making purchases, and the nature of their buying motives should be major determinants of nonprice competitive strategy. In addition, the complexity of the product is likely to

Figure I–1

RELATIVE IMPORTANCE OF THE MAJOR
ELEMENTS OF THE MARKETING MIX

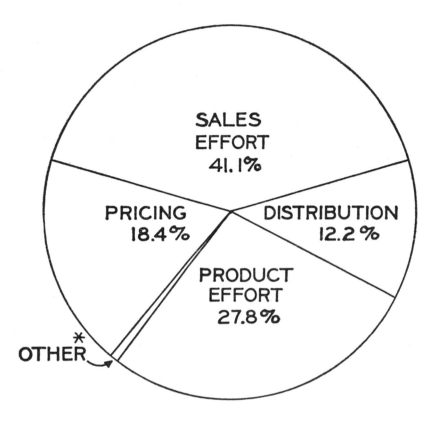

*Total marketing strategy is 100 percent. Respondents allocated 0.5 percent of their strategy to activities other than price, product, sales and distribution.

be influential. The expected relationship between these attributes of a product-market and competitive strategy is as follows:

1. *The relative importance of product effort should vary directly with the strength of operational buying motives, the purchasing efforts and the knowledge of the buyer, and the technical nature of the product.*

2. *The relative importance of sales effort should vary directly with the strength of socio-psychological buying motives, while varying inversely with the purchasing efforts and knowledge of the buyer and the technical nature of the product.*

If these hypotheses are correct, the relative importance of the product facet of competitive strategy should be greatest among industrial goods producers and least among producers of consumer nondurable goods. Using a semantic differential, measurements of the product-market attributes (as perceived by the respondents) were obtained. It was found that industrial buyers tended to have predominantly operational buying motives, more extensive buying efforts, and more knowledge concerning products than the purchasers of consumer goods. In addition, the average industrial good was considered more technical than the average consumer good.

As shown in Table I-1, industrial goods producers allocated 30

Table I–1

PERCEIVED IMPORTANCE OF MAJOR FACETS OF COMPETITIVE STRATEGY IN VARIOUS INDUSTRIES*

Facet	Industrial Goods	Consumer Durables	Consumer Nondurables
Sales Effort	40.9	37.5	44.7
Distribution	10.1	18.7	16.3
Product Effect	29.6	24.3	22.8
Pricing	19.0	19.0	16.0
Other	.4	.5	.2
Total	100.0	100.0	100.0
Total of Sales Efforts & Distribution	51.0	56.2	61.0

*The data are the average point allocations of 344 industrial, 52 consumer durable, and 89 consumer nondurable goods manufacturers.

[6]

points to product effort while producers of consumer durables and nondurables allocated 24 and 23 points, respectively. Therefore, the allocation of points supports the hypothesis that the relative importance of product effort will increase with the technical nature of the product, the dominance of operational buying motives, the efforts of the buyer, and the knowledge of the buyer.

If the sales effort hypothesis is correct, one would expect marketing communications to be most important in the sale of consumer goods, especially consumer nondurables. The 45 points allocated to sales effort by manufacturers of consumer nondurables were greater than the 41 points allocated by producers of industrial goods and the 38 points allocated by consumer durable goods producers. Another test of the hypothesis is provided by combining sales effort and distribution because total sales effort would include the selection and development of distribution channels. When combined, one finds that manufacturers of consumer nondurables allocated 61 points to marketing communications and distribution, durable goods producers allocated 56 points, and industrial goods producers allocated 51 points. Therefore, the data indicate that the importance of sales effort does vary directly with the strength of socio-psychological buying motives and inversely with the purchasing effort and knowledge of the buyer and the technical nature of the product.

Using the product and sales effort hypotheses, a decision model for nonprice competitive strategy is developed in Chapter V. Also presented is a detailed evaluation of the role of each attribute of a firm's product-market. At this point we shall simply summarize that model by stating that the importance of the product facet of marketing strategy varies directly with the sophistication of the product-market. A sophisticated product-market is one where:

1. Buyers' knowledge concerning the product and its want-satisfying power is great.

2. Buyers' efforts to make a wise purchase are substantial.

3. Motives for purchasing the product are operational rather than socio-psychological in nature.

[7]

4. Product complexity, from the purchaser's point of view, is substantial.

On the other hand, the importance of sales effort varies inversely with the sophistication of the product-market.

In evaluating the above model, the marketing strategies of several industrial and consumer goods industries are examined. As predicted by the model, aerospace and defense contractors place the greatest reliance on product effort, while producers of consumer petroleum products place the least. Sales effort receives its greatest emphasis in the strategy of the petroleum producers, and the least emphasis among aerospace and defense contractors.

Specific Strategies Vary Markedly

The importance of the various elements of each major facet of marketing strategy varied dramatically from one industry to another. However, *the most important competitive activity for almost all types of manufacturers was sales management and personal selling.* Over 28 percent of the total strategy of successful producers of industrial goods was attributed to this element of the marketing mix. Among the manufacturers of consumer nondurable goods, only 17 percent of the total strategy was allocated to sales management and personal selling, but it was still perceived to be the most important element of their products' success.

Considering only the nonprice activities, product service and technical R & D were second and third in importance for industrial goods producers. Manufacturers of consumer durables rated development of the channel of distribution and advertising as second and third in importance. Advertising was almost as important as sales management among the consumer nondurable goods producers. These respondents rated technical R & D as third in importance; however, it was only slightly more important than the development of the channel of distribution.

If pricing is not subdivided into specific categories of activities, as were the other major facets of strategy, it is visualized as second in importance to industrial goods manufacturers and first in importance to producers of consumer goods.

The variety in the nature of marketing strategies is even greater

[8]

among more specific industries. This is illustrated by the differences between the marketing strategies of aerospace and defense contractors and producers of consumer petroleum products.

Table I–2

DIFFERENCES IN THE MARKETING STRATEGIES OF TWO INDUSTRIES

	Perceived Importance of Each Activity in:	
Marketing Activity	Aerospace & Defense	Consumer Petroleum Products
Sales Management and Personal Selling	19.6	22.0
Advertising	3.0	12.2
Other Sales Efforts	3.7	11.9
Determination, Selection & Development of Distribution Channels	.5	9.3
Physical Distribution	.8	8.8
Product Service	16.3	4.8
Technical R & D	24.6	6.2
Other Product Efforts	9.0	4.4
Pricing According to Competitive Levels	3.2	15.6
Other Pricing Strategies	18.4	5.0
Other Marketing Activities	1.0	.0
Total Marketing Strategy	100.0*	100.0*

*Total may not exactly equal 100.0 because of the rounding of individual values.

As indicated in Table I-2, advertising is four times more important to producers of petroleum products than to companies in the aerospace and defense industry. All other sales effort activities are also more important to the petroleum producers.

Activities relating to channels of distribution are almost 19 times more important to the petroleum industry than to the aerospace and defense contractors. Physical distribution is perceived as eleven times more important by the petroleum products producers.

Product service is over three times more important, and technical R & D is four times more important, to aerospace and defense contractors than to petroleum producers.

Pricing is about equally important to both groups, but the producers of consumer petroleum products place a great emphasis on pricing according to competitive levels while the aerospace and defense contractors emphasize other pricing strategies.

These differences vividly illustrate how greatly marketing strategies vary from one industry to another. They also illus-

trate the need for a conceptual model that will aid executives in developing marketing strategies that are appropriate for the products that they administer.

Market Structure Not Influential

Upon examining relative positions in the market, as measured by the share of market and sales volume of each company, there appears to be little relationship between the emphasis placed on the various facets of competitive strategy and market structure. In other words, the importance of each facet is, at best, only slightly related to the share of market or sales volume of a company's product.

Marketing Costs

Distinct differences exist in the marketing costs of various industries, with costs tending to vary inversely with the sophistication of the product-market. Median marketing costs ranged from four percent among aerospace and defense contractors to 20 percent among producers of consumer nondurable goods. About equally large differences occurred among products with various sales volumes. Products with sales of less than $500,000 had median marketing costs of 23 percent, while those with sales of over $10,000,000 had median marketing costs which were only eight percent of total costs. There was almost no relationship between marketing costs and share of market, and the median marketing cost of all firms was ten percent.

Conclusion

While price, product and sales efforts are all indispensible and vitally important elements of the marketing mix, the nonprice elements are of major significance in the strategies of modern industry. There appears to be, at most, only a slight relationship between the importance of the nonprice elements and the size and market share of a company. On the other hand, there is a definite relationship between the perceived importance of product and sales efforts facets and the behavioral characteristics of the product-market.

More specifically, the relative importance of product effort varies directly with the purchasing efforts and knowledge of the

buyer, the technical nature of the product, and the strength of operational buying motives. The significance of sales effort in the marketing mix varies inversely with the technical nature of the product, purchasing efforts and knowledge of the buyer, while varying directly with the strength of socio-psychological buying motives.

Although the above conceptual guidelines are general in nature, they are capable of explaining many of the differences in the marketing strategies of a wide range of successful products in American industry.

While the product-market model and information on 485 marketing strategies can be useful in the evaluation of current strategies and the design of improved marketing programs, the greatest potential benefit of the product-market model lies in its philosophical implications. To design efficient and effective competitive strategies, management must create marketing programs that are consonant or in harmony with the nature of the product and, more important, the behavioral characteristics of its potential market. Not only should the knowledge, purchasing efforts, and motivation of the buyer be considered, but so should any other behavioral characteristic that is prominent in the purchase of the product.

CHAPTER II

THE ROLE OF SCIENCE AND THEORY
IN BUSINESS

Science, like business, is a speculative enterprise. Both the scientist and the business executive operate in a world of uncertainty. Similarly, the efforts of each may result in success or failure, and even when successful, the results are likely to be far from perfect.

Some writers prefer to define science as a coordinated body of knowledge meeting a number of criteria such as internal consistency and predictability.[1] However, it is more useful to visualize science as *the process of objectively and systematically searching for truth.* The product of successful scientific search is a systematic body of knowledge organized around one or more central themes.

Business administration is usually perceived as being primarily an art, rather than a science, and there is no large body of systematized business knowledge. However, every science, no matter how elaborately developed, had a rudimentary beginning. Therefore, there is a science of business so long as there are those engaged in a systematic and objective search for useful generalizations and truth concerning the management and behavior of the business enterprise.

Scientific Endeavor Produces Theory

The knowledge resulting from science is comprised of theories which are internally consistent and have been validated empirically. Baumol visualizes theory as a systematic explanation, as a structure which describes the functioning and interrelations of some phenomenon.[2] A theory is usually developed by examining

[1] For an excellent example, see R. D. Buzzell, "Is Marketing a Science?" *Harvard Business Review*, XLI (January, 1963), pp. 32-40.
[2] W. S. Baumol, "On the Role of Marketing Theory," *Journal of Marketing*, XXI (April, 1957), p. 413.

some aspect of reality and constructing a simplified model (consisting of one or more hypotheses) which behaves, in general, like the reality under observation. Such a theory is considered useful if it enables one to accurately predict nonobvious conclusions.

A hypothesis is an *untested* explanation or description of some phenomenon. It is, at best, a proposed explanation or belief to be tested by experimentation and empirical evidence. The hypothesis, or model, is accepted as theory if it is testable—simple enough to permit systematic manipulation and analysis—*and*, if the predictions of the model are sufficiently accurate to be useful.

To be most effective, a theory of business behavior should be pragmatically oriented. It should be grounded in reality and potentially useful to business management, government administrators, or consumers. Therefore, business theory should be visualized as an instrument for making decisions which are superior to those made without the benefit of a theoretical foundation.

Unfortunately, there are few useful theories of business behavior. The business manager usually does not have a pragmatic conceptual foundation for defining and evaluating various alternative courses of action. Business, however, is not in an uncrowded boat. Most of the social sciences are not endowed with a well-developed and internally consistent body of theory. Social sciences, business included, suffer from the difficulty that the object of their study is highly complex Homo sapiens who cannot realistically be manipulated and controlled in the artificial environment of a laboratory.

The most well-developed body of social science theory is found in economics; however, one can question whether the classical, neo-classical and other theories of economics can, with reasonable accuracy, predict nonobvious conclusions. These theories often depart so far from the twentieth century reality that they are frequently of limited use to the decision-maker.

The classical models of the firm did constitute reasonable and useful approximations of *eighteenth century* business behavior, and provided an analytical framework for the study and prediction of relationships among economic variables. Unfortunately, much of the reality they dealt with has since changed substantially. Despite this limitation, economics is, relative to most other

[14]

social sciences, well endowed with useful theories. For example, several additions have been made to the classical models of firm behavior which have helped to preserve their usefulness in the rapidly changing environment of the twentieth century. Concepts such as limit (pre-emptive) pricing and the condition of entry, the kinked oligopoly curve, and other modifications have helped to update the pricing models of the classical tradition and have made economics a living science.

The Need For Theory In Business

While business is not a well-developed science with a systematic body of knowledge, the need for scientific endeavor and the resulting theory is indeed great. Furthermore, this need will expand substantially in the years ahead. As businesses grow in size and share of market, the social consequence of their actions becomes increasingly great. The results of a single decision can mean millions of dollars in gain or loss to the business firm. Moreover, a major decision by one company may have a multi-million dollar impact on other firms and the total economy because of the interdependence of business firms in a highly developed economy. For example, the pricing and production decisions of Henry Ford leading to the creation of a mass market for automobiles, and the product decisions of Dupont leading to the development of nylon and other synthetic fibers, have had a profound influence on industry and society the world over.

Decisions concerning products, investments, pricing, marketing communications, and production should not be made without the benefit of a realistic and useful theoretical foundation. Management needs to be able to predict the future impact of its major decisions on the company, competitors, customers, suppliers, and society. Because of a lack of appropriate theory, it is frequently difficult to predict the consequences of many business decisions on even one of these major parties, to say nothing of all of them.

Government also needs an appropriate theoretical foundation for evaluating business behavior. The historical foundation for most of our antitrust laws and their enforcement has been the classical theories of competition and monopoly. However, these theories are based on assumptions that do not adequately explain

the economic behavior of the most prevalent type of business organization in the United States—oligopoly. A major aspect of this deficiency is the inability of the classical approach to realistically incorporate the role of product and sales efforts into a theory of competitive behavior.

The result of such deficiencies is considerable confusion and uncertainty among antitrusters, the courts, and businessmen. This confusion breeds conflict. For example, Donald F. Turner, former Harvard professor and recent head of the Antitrust Division of the U. S. Department of Justice, has stated, "I believe that advertising has significantly adverse effects on competition in consumer goods markets to be an appropriate subject for concern."[3] More recently, a study by the FTC has condemned the nation's major oil companies for spending increased amounts of money on promotional advertising instead of lowering prices to consumers.[4] In response to Turner, Stanford Smith, General Manager of the American Newspaper Publishers Association, has stated, "The very essence of advertising is competition. It is inconceivable that one can be for competition and against advertising." His thesis is supported by the research of economist Jules Backman.[5]

Conflicts such as these arise because of the lack of a theoretical foundation for ordering the facts and determining the economic consequences of advertising and other dimensions of competitive behavior. The ultimate resolution of these conflicts is likely to have a profound influence on business, the economic system, and society. Unless an appropriate theory of business and competitive behavior is developed, many mistakes may be made at the expense of private enterprise and the public which it serves.

A logical starting point in the quest for a theoretical foundation is to briefly review the historical development of the theory of competitive behavior.

---

[3] "Advertising: A Reassuring Antitrust Word," *New York Times,* February 9, 1967.
[4] "FTC Report Critical of Gasoline Gimmicks," *Wisconsin State Journal,* June 30, 1967.
[5] Jules Backman, *Advertising and Competition* (New York: New York University Press, 1967).

Classical Approach To The Problems Of Competitive Strategy

The great attraction of the classical competitive price theory lies in its simplicity and determinateness. A horizontal demand curve and a U-shaped cost curve are assumed for each supplier, as are a large number of buyers and sellers, perfect knowledge, homogeneous products, the freedom of entry and exit to and from the industry, and profit maximization as the entrepreneur's sole motivation. In this setting, quantity is the only variable of competitive behavior,[6] and the unique solution—what price and quantity—is merely the logical outcome of the assumed impersonal market forces.

Perhaps this theory of perfect competition was a satisfactory explanation of firm behavior in the agricultural economy of the nineteenth century. But even in the days of Ricardo, Marshall, and Edgeworth, economists were aware of the existence of imperfectly competitive markets. Most theorists preferred to treat such cases as unexplained exceptions, or to dismiss them by treating imperfect competition as monopoly. Only a few were courageous enough to tackle the theory of firm behavior in an imperfectly competitive market structure.

One of the earliest, Cournot, in 1838, attempted to solve the problem of duopoly[7] by specifying that each duopolist would ignore his mutual dependence and assume his rival's supply as constant.[8] A duopolist, therefore, could compute the quantity and price which would maximize his profits by deducting his rival's output from the total industry demand and thereby derive his own demand curve. It is unnecessary to elaborate on this approach because it was unsuccessful. Although an interesting attempt, it was naive in that each rival assumed the other rival's quantity would be constant regardless of his own output and price. Because of this assumption, the theory lacked both realism

---

[6] The assumption of perfect knowledge eliminates both the need for and the economic feasibility of sales promotion, while the assumption of product homogeneity eliminates the possibility of product differentiation.

[7] An industry consisting of two firms.

[8] Antoine Cournot, *Recherches sur les Principles Mathematiques de la Theorie des Richesses* (Paris: 1838), Chapter 7.

and predictive power.[9]

Others followed Cournot's footsteps in an attempt to solve the duopoly (and oligopoly) problem. Most notable are the efforts of Bertrand[10] in 1883 and Edgeworth[11] in 1897. The basic weakness of their theories was essentially the same as Cournot's—they assumed that firms would not recognize their interdependence. However, Bertrand and Edgeworth assumed it was the rival's price that was constant. Each firm, therefore, would not realize that its behavior would influence the prices set by its rival. Again the assumption, although different from Cournot's, was unrealistic and the resulting theories lacked the ability to explain and predict the behavior of the duopolist.[12]

In the early 1930's, the "father" and "mother" of imperfect competition theory, Edward Chamberlin and Joan Robinson, introduced a new dimension into the theory of firm behavior—the role of product differentiation and the resulting monopolistic competition.[13] Their works were substantially similar, so the brief discussion to follow shall be limited to Chamberlin's contribution.

Chamberlin argued that theory of monopoly seems adequate to explain the pricing of differentiated products. This conclusion was based upon the grounds that (1) real or fancied differences exist among the goods of many sellers,[14] and (2) the essence of monopoly is control over supply.[15] Therefore, any firm having a differentiated product is a monopolist in the sense that it has exclusive control over its own differentiated product. Monopoly, however, is only Chamberlin's opening wedge; competition still exists because differentiated products may be substituted for one another. Consequently, he arrived at a market situation which is descriptively labeled "monopolistic competition."[16]

---

[9] The interested reader may find a more detailed exposition and criticism of Cournot's theory in William Fellner's *Competition Among the Few* (New York: Augustus M. Kelly, 1960), Chapter 2.

[10] Joseph Bertrand, *Journal des Savats* (Paris: 1883), p. 503.

[11] F. Y. Edgeworth, "La Teoria Pura del Monopolio," *Giornale degli Economists*, Vol. XV (1897). A translation into English appears in his *Papers Relating to Political Economy*, Vol. I (London: Macmillan & Co., 1925), p. 111.

[12] A brief explanation and criticism of the works of Bertrand and Edgeworth may be found in Edward H. Chamberlin's *The Theory of Monopolistic Competition*, 7th ed. (Cambridge: Harvard University Press, 1958), pp. 34-46.

[13] Chamberlin, *op. cit.*, and Joan Robinson, *The Economics of Imperfect Competition* (London: Macmillan and Company, 1934).

[14] Chamberlin, *op. cit.*, p. 56.

[15] *Ibid.*, p. 65.

[16] *Ibid.*, pp. 68-70.

Chamberlin described the monopolistically competitive firm's sales as limited and defined by three factors controllable by the firm:[17] (1) price, (2) the nature of the product, and (3) advertising outlays. The goal of the firm is to adjust these variables in a manner which will maximize profits. This adjustment, however, is complicated by competition and interdependence with rival firms producing substitute products. With his new twist, product differentiation and monopolistic competition, Chamberlin resorted to the classical equilibrium approach in working out a theoretical solution. His basic model of the monopolistically competitive firm centered on the "heroic assumption that both demand and cost curves for all the 'products' are uniform throughout the group."[18] Two demand curves were involved, one based upon the assumption that rivals' prices are constant, and the other assuming that rivals' prices are always identical to that charged by the firm.[19] Using the classical equilibrium approach and a number of unrealistic assumptions (such as symmetrical cost curves), Chamberlin's theoretical analysis might be described as a very fruitful failure. The attempt was fruitful in that it led to a reorientation of economic thinking and provided the incentive for empirical research on the nature of competition. Thus, Chamberlin brought monopolistic competition into the limelight of economic analysis,[20] and the question of the importance of variables other than price (product differentiation, firm recognition of interdependence, advertising, and the threat of potential entry) was raised. Nevertheless, the strong tradition of price theory centering around a definite, long-term equilibrium price made the idea of indeterminateness repulsive to Chamberlin, and most of his analysis concentrated on those cases where determinate solutions could be achieved. This was done by making the impersonal market forces the controlling factors and limiting the independent action of the firm to an adjustment to these forces.[21] In short, Chamberlin, like all before him,

---

[17] *Ibid.*, p. 71.
[18] *Ibid.*, p. 82.
[19] *Ibid.*, p. 90.
[20] Whereas previous to this time theoretical analysis regarded it as the exception.
[21] A typical Chamberlinian case assumes a market characterized by many small producers and freedom of entry—both factors seriously limiting the individual firm's freedom of action.

failed to present a theoretical analysis which adequately explained the role of the variables he had hoped to add to the classical model of firm behavior.

Other economists, stimulated by the efforts of Chamberlin and Robinson, have attempted to add these and other variables to the theory of the firm. A major contributor, Joe S. Bain, has emphasized the concept of limit pricing and the condition of entry.[22] He realistically points out that it may be to the firm's advantage to take less than maximum profits today in the hope that potential competitors will be discouraged from entering the market and driving down the prices and profits of tomorrow. Therefore, the firm may limit its present prices to an amount less than the short-run profit maximizing price to keep potential competitors out of the industry. Whether a firm will do this, and to what extent the price will be limited, is dependent upon the condition (or ease) of entry into the industry. Bain also attempted to classify the various possible market structures according to how each will affect firm behavior and what the social consequence of this behavior will be.[23]

A presentation of the many other contributions prompted by Chamberlin and Robinson is not feasible. Among them are the works of Sweezy, Stigler, Rothschild, Brems, Fellner, Abbott, and Baumol. The purpose of this brief review is only to (1) introduce the problem of explaining the behavior of the firm in an imperfect market structure, and (2) recall the type of approach that has been taken by economists in their attempts to solve this problem.[24] Two general conclusions can be drawn. First, economists have traditionally emphasized pricing over the other facets of competitive behavior. Second, the majority of theoretical attempts to explain both price and nonprice behavior have relied upon the impersonal market structure of the industry (e.g., perfectly competitive, duopolistic, monopolistic) .

---

[22] Joe S. Bain, *Barriers to New Competition* (Cambridge: Harvard University Press, 1956), pp. 1-42.

[23] Bain, *Pricing, Distribution, and Employment* (New York: Henry Holt and Company, 1958).

[24] The interested reader who is not familiar with this historical development may refer to the original writings which have been listed in the footnotes of this chapter, especially Fellner's *Competition Among the Few*, Chamberlin's *Monopolistic Competition*, and Bain's *Pricing, Distribution, and Employment*. For other significant contributions which have not been mentioned, the reader is referred to the Bibliography.

[20]

Requirements For A Modern Approach

Certainly the behavior of the firm is influenced by the size and number of its competitors, the degree of recognition of interdependence, the condition of entry into the industry, the amount of collusion among rivals, and other factors which have been emphasized by the classical and neo-classical economists. Bringing these factors into the theory of competitive behavior is necessary and fruitful (particularly in explaining pricing behavior), but these factors alone do not explain *how* a firm will, or should, compete for the buyer's patronage. Business management sometimes chooses to emphasize the nonprice facets of competitive strategy—namely, product differentiation and sales efforts. This emphasis does not imply that pricing is unimportant; it is and always will be important so long as we have quasi-free enterprise economies. However, the nonprice facets of competition may often be more important than pricing in the marketing strategy of the firm—a hypothesis to be empirically tested in Chapter V.

The second major hypothesis to be evaluated is that a theory of nonprice competitive strategy, to be realistic and useful, must take into consideration the nature of a firm's product, and more important, the characteristics of the potential buyers of the product. For example, one would not expect a producer of newsprint (an industrial good used primarily by newspapers) to compete in a manner identical to a producer of perfume simply because the market structures of their industries happen to be similar. To explain and predict nonprice competitive strategy, behavioral variables must be added to the economic models. Therefore, the primary objective of this book is to suggest and test a realistic, conceptual foundation for explaining and predicting the nonprice competitive strategy of a business within today's social and economic environment.

CHAPTER III

IMPACT OF A DYNAMIC ENVIRONMENT

In order to be understood, an economic theory must be interpreted in light of the social and economic setting in which it originated and was to be applied. Classical economic theory was the product of eighteenth and nineteenth century European economists. If one looks back to the economic environment of their day, the theory of competition and monopoly has great merit despite its inability to deal with the imperfectly competitive market situation.

The Environment Of Classical Economics

In the subsistence economies of the eighteenth and nineteenth centuries, a nation's greatest economic problem was to obtain the necessities for survival. Economic activity was almost entirely devoted to producing the goods and services needed to satisfy minimal needs and comforts. The history of all nations has been characterized by this struggle of consumers to satisfy their immediate needs for food, clothing, housing, drugs, and other necessities. Several nations, such as Peru, are still very much involved in this struggle. The economic environment of the classical tradition may be characterized by four related phenomena:

    I. Scarcity of Resources
        Herein lies the foundation of economic activity
        and economic analysis.[1] Without the scarcity of

---

[1] Economics is defined by George S. Stigler as "the study of the principles governing the allocation of scarce means among competing ends when the objective of the allocation is to maximize the attainment of the ends." *Theory of Price* (New York: The Macmillan Co., 1946).

goods, and the necessity of allocating them among individuals, there would be no economic problems. As indicated above, the problem of scarcity was acute in the eighteenth and nineteenth centuries. The second characteristic of the environment of classical economists was directly related to this scarcity.

II. Low Consumer Incomes

Historically, almost all societies have had a number of wealthy consumers such as the pharoahs of Egypt, the czars of Russia, the kings and landlords of the European feudal system, and the governors, traders, and large landholders of early America. These, however, were the privileged few, whereas the majority of society had barely enough income to purchase a mediocre standard of living. This was the condition of the masses at the time the classical approach was originated.

III. A Seller's Market

Both the scarcity of resources and low consumer incomes lead to this third basic characteristic. The seller's market was so strong that a Frenchman by the name of Jean Baptiste Say (1767-1832) went so far as to build a theory of "debouches" (markets) on the assumption that there can be no general overproduction of goods.[2] Say's Law rested upon the premise that goods are bought with other goods. Since the whole economy is based on exchange, the creation of one product opens the vent for other products. Therefore, the general over-production of goods would be impossible. In essence, Say argued that consumer spending is a function of income, tied to it by an iron law because most, if not all, of a consumer's income would be expended in providing the necessities of life. Since production created those necessities, and in so doing provided purchasing power, production generates its own

---

[2] Jean Baptiste Say, *A Treatise on Political Economy* (Paris: 1803).

market. This view became an integral part of the classical tradition and is one reason for the production orientation of that tradition.

IV. Few Economies of Large Scale

The technology of the eighteenth and nineteenth centuries was relatively simple. Most products were agriculturally oriented and there were few advantages to large units of production, even though such units sometimes existed, such as the large farms of feudal landlords. Manufacturing was primarily performed by individual craftsmen or small aggregations of laborers. Shoemakers, candlemakers, blacksmiths, carpenters, and similar craftsmen produced most of the manufactured goods which were exchanged in the marketplace. In addition, many goods were made and consumed within individual households.

This was, in brief, the economic world of the classical economists. In addition to the scarcity of resources, low consumer incomes, the seller's market, and simple technology there prevailed a "laissez-faire" philosophy of government. Although there was not an entire absence of government restrictions on business, government regulation was, by present standards, at a low level. As for the entrepreneur, his philosophy was "caveat emptor"—let the buyer beware—while the firm used the scarce resources it controlled to its own advantage.

In this setting competition provided, as it does today, the key to protection of the consumer in a capitalistic economy. But what is competition and what constitutes competitive behavior? The classicist defined competition, in terms of the structure of the industry, i.e., an industry with such a large number of buyers and sellers that no one party could exercise any control over the market.[3] Competitive behavior, which would lead an industry to the state of perfect competitive equilibrium, centered around price.

In contrast, economists today concede that competitive be-

[3] For other assumptions of the Classical Competitive Theory, see Chapter II, p. 17.

[25]

havior has three major facets: product differentiation, sales promotion, and price. In the economy of the classicists, product differentiation was not very important as a means of competition. The competing products of an industry within any market area were simple in nature. Most of the product differences which did exist were readily ascertainable by inspection and were priced accordingly. Product differentiation and competition through product improvement were not, relative to pricing, important aspects of competitive behavior.

Sales promotion, outside of some simple conveyance of information, was also almost nonexistent. Simple, undifferentiated products provided little basis for sales promotion. In addition, production was on a small scale basis, and mass sales efforts were not needed. The scarcity of resources was another reason for the lack of sales promotion (and the lack of product differentiation). In short, the consumption of resources for sales promotion was considered highly unproductive in an economy where buyers were attempting to satisfy essential needs.

For all practical purposes, this left pricing as the sole important parameter or facet of competitive behavior and the key to the welfare of the consumer. It is easy to understand the central role of the market structure in the early classical theory of competition. Because of the lack of government regulation, the scarcity of resources, the low consumer incomes, and the resulting *seller's market,* the control of a market by one firm could easily be used for the monopolist's advantage at society's expense. With "caveat emptor" as his philosophy, the monopolist would limit production and raise prices in the effort to maximize profits. It is not difficult to visualize why the perfectly competitive market structure was so admired.

The Environment Of Today's Advanced Economies

With the advancement of technology and the resulting transformation to a modern industrial economy, the economic environment of the advanced nations of the world is drastically different from that of the classical economist. The economy of the 1970s may be characterized as follows:

    I. Greater Abundance of Resources (in relation to needs)

[26]

IMPACT OF A DYNAMIC ENVIRONMENT

Newly discovered mineral deposits, improved extraction and refining processes, synthetic materials, dramatic improvements in agriculture, and advancements in manufacturing have transformed the United States and other prosperous nations into societies of abundance. Instead of a shortage of food, one of the most plaguing economic and political problems of the United States is an ability to produce too much wheat, corn, cotton, and other agricultural produce. In response to this problem, the U. S. Department of Agriculture spends billions of dollars annually to support prices and pay farmers for not using their productive resources.

This overcapacity has also been present in manufacturing industries. In recent years, the steel, paper, oil, and automobile industries have often operated at well under full capacity. In fact, the totality of U. S. industry rarely operates at over 90 percent of rated capacity and sometimes utilizes less than 75 percent of total capacity.[4]

By emphasizing overcapacity and an abundance of resources, it is not implied that resources are abundant in relation to the *desires* of man, or that everyone's needs have been met. However, it is implied that resources are abundant in relation to man's physical needs in the United States and numerous other countries.

II. High Consumer Incomes

The economies of the advanced nations have undergone an income revolution. With advancing technology and increased productivity, these economies have grown wealthy. Because of government taxation and numerous social and economic forces, this wealth has been quite widely dispersed. The result is broad middle and upper-middle income groups, rather than masses of poor people and a few who

---

[4] U. S. Department of Commerce, *Statistical Abstract of the United States* (Washington, D.C.: Government Printing Office, 1969), p. 714.

are rich. For example, more than two-thirds of all U. S. families have annual incomes above $7,000, and approximately 50 percent have incomes above $10,000. A considerable proportion of these incomes is discretionary. That is, it is available for purchases (or saving) other than those necessary for physical survival. The existence of discretionary income has made possible the huge market for recreational goods such as snowmobiles, hunting and fishing equipment, boats, campers, and other products.

III. A Buyer's Market

The increasing substitutability of various products has tended to reduce the ability of any one producer or group of producers (such as a specific industry) to exert a significant degree of monopolistic control. This is indeed fortunate, given the economies of large scale and the rising concentration of industry in manufacturing. Even the large oligopolists of the steel industry are often faced with substantial competition because of the existence of substitute materials such as aluminum, fiberglass, plastic, and in some instances (such as building materials), wood, paper, concrete, and other alternatives. Because of the technological advances which have produced this rising substitutability, the rising concentration of manufacturing industry and the emergence of oligopolistic market structures usually have not preserved seller's markets. Instead, the third major characteristic of the U. S. economy is the emergence of a buyer's market.

The abundance of resources, the growth of wealth and disposable income, and the substitutability of products have all contributed to an increased freedom of buyers to select from a vast variety of products and services. As a result, consumers have a powerful voice in the economy. This does not deny the possible existence of a seller's market in some industries (the medical services industry might be characterized as such). However, the economic

developments outlined above have eliminated most of the seller's markets and replaced them with buyer's markets.

The typical consumer not only has the political freedom to buy what he pleases and several alternatives from which to select, but he also has the purchasing power to enable him to capitalize on this freedom. George Romney, former president of American Motors Corporation, later governor of Michigan and then Secretary of the U. S. Department of Housing and Urban Development, has suggested the use of the word *consumerism* in place of *capitalism* as a more accurate description of America's economic system.

He points out that the American people, in their role as consumers, are "the real bosses" of the economy. A company's success, according to Mr. Romney, depends upon its ability to produce products that meet the needs and desires of the buying public.[5]

Although the substitution of the word consumerism for capitalism may be going too far, there is merit in what Mr. Romney says. The market often is a buyer's market and the seller, to be successful, must cater to the needs and desires of the buyer.

IV. Economies of Large Scale

A fourth major characteristic of modern economic life is the increasing prevalence of economies of large scale, especially in manufacturing and agriculture. The division and specialization of labor and the emergence of a massive technology have produced economies of scale in both production and marketing. For example, the rise of mass communications enables sellers to deliver thousands of messages concerning their wares to millions of individual homes each day.

[5] George Romney, "The Compact Car Revolution—A Case History in Consumerism," *Michigan Business Review,* II (July, 1959) pp. 1-7.

The consequence of economies of large scale has been a dramatic increase in the productivity and size of units of production and distribution. In most industries, the number of firms necessary to constitute a perfectly competitive market structure would be highly inefficient and economically undesirable.

In addition to the economic changes in today's business environment, there have been a large number of political alterations. In the United States, the present system of anti-trust laws, trade regulations, and congressional investigations is far removed from the "laissez-faire" political system advocated by Adam Smith and his followers.[6] Although today's firm still operates within a predominantly capitalistic economic system, its freedom is severely limited by government regulations and controls.

In this environment of public controls, abundant resources, many wealthy consumers, a buyer's market and economies of large scale, competition can no longer be described in terms of a large number of firms offering homogeneous products to buyers with perfect knowledge. Nor can the theory of competitive behavior be restricted to pricing. If the theory of competition and firm action is to be a predictive and useful tool, it must recognize that competition is no longer limited to the rivalry between the identical products of a specific industry. In the eighteenth and nineteenth centuries, competition was between firms producing like products needed by consumers. *But today, competition is between firms producing diverse products needing customers. In essence, competition is direct rivalry for the consumer's dollar.*[7] The firm, in competing for a share of this dol-

---

[6] See Adam Smith's *Wealth of Nations,* Book V (New York: Random House, Inc., 1937).

[7] The word direct is used because all goods are in indirect competition for the consumer's dollar. This indirect rivalry would not provide the consumer the economic protection he needs in a free enterprise economy. Direct rivalry does afford economic protection, provided sellers compete fairly, vigorously, and without collusion.

lar, is often in direct rivalry with firms of many industries in addition to the other firms of its own industry. For example, the producer of glass containers is not only in competition with other glass producers, but is often in vigorous competition with producers of aluminum, plastics, tin, paper, and even wood on some occasions. A manufacturer of sports cars may be in competition with boat manufacturers, vacation trips, furniture, and many other producers, depending upon the preference scale of each potential customer. For example, an unmarried university graduate, upon obtaining his first employment and a few paychecks, might consider the purchase of some commodity which would offer both summer enjoyment and social prestige in appealing to the opposite sex. One possibility would be to trade in his five-year-old sedan on a new, bright red convertible. A highly competitive second alternative would be to keep his present automobile and purchase a high-powered speedboat. Both alternatives, the new convertible and the speedboat, offer similar satisfactions—summer enjoyment and social prestige.

Chamberlin and other present-day economists have recognized this inter-industry competition and the role of selling costs, product differentiation, and government regulations. And yet, as pointed out in Chapter I, most have persisted in attempting to relate price and nonprice behavior to the market structure of a specific industry. *As a result, the typical contribution is the simple acknowledgment that product differentiation and selling efforts exist, and that their existence may make the demand curve less elastic or shift it to the right.* Economists have found it convenient to assume that these two major aspects of competitive behavior are constant. They can then proceed with the traditional analysis of U-shaped cost curves and a given demand curve with the result that pricing behavior is dependent upon the market structure of the industry. In any

event, they have not provided a realistic theory of nonprice competitive behavior.

Implications For Marketing Management

The magnitude of this shortcoming is illustrated by a study conducted during the spring of 1958. At that time the author became interested in the question, "What areas of management are most crucial to a firm's marketing success?"[8] In an attempt to find the answer, a questionnaire was sent to the marketing directors of 244 successful manufacturing firms.[9] Management's interest in the study was reflected by a 75 percent response within an eight-week period.

The first section of the questionnaire listed 12 general policy areas of marketing management, (e.g., pricing, advertising and sales promotion, and product service). The respondent, usually the vice-president or director of marketing, was asked to select the five areas which he regarded as most important in his company's marketing success.

The response to this fairly rough measuring device[10] indicates that product research and development, with a 78.5 percent selection ratio, is most important in modern day competitive strategy. Ranking second is sales research and sales planning with a 73 percent selection ratio. Ranking third is the management of sales personnel, 58 percent; fourth, advertising and sales promotion, 56 percent; fifth, product service, 52 percent; and sixth, pricing, with less than a 50 percent selection ratio. Table III-1 presents a percentage analysis of the responses.

---

[8] Marketing is herein defined as the activities of business rivalry, which consist primarily of the planning, pricing, promotion, distribution, and servicing of the goods and services desired by consumers.

[9] Selecting a sample of well-managed and successful manufacturing companies presented a major problem in the study. The use of *Martindell's Manual of Excellent Management—1957* provided an efficient solution. Martindell heads a management consulting firm which publishes an annual listing of well-managed companies based upon the point system of evaluation developed by his American Institute of Management.

[10] Each of the five selected policy areas receive equal weight in the computations; therefore, the ranking obtained are not precise measurements of the relative importance of the various policy areas.

Table III–1

HOW MANAGEMENT PERCEIVES THE ELEMENTS
OF MARKETING SUCCESS

Rank	Policy Area	Percent of Firms Selecting the Policy Area
1	Product Research and Development	78.5
2	Sales Research and Sales Planning	73.3
3	Management of Sales Personnel	58.5
4	Advertising and Sales Promotion	55.6
5	Product Service	51.9
6	Pricing	49.6
7	Organizational Structure	43.7
8	Distribution Channels and Their Control	40.7
9	Marketing Cost Budgeting and Control	17.0
10	Financing and Credit	14.1
11	Transportation and Storage	6.7
12	Public Relations	6.7

Source: 135 producer's questionnaires.

The relative unimportance ascribed to pricing is of interest. Since the study was conducted in a period of business recession, it seems reasonable to assume that this should have introduced a bias in favor of the importance of pricing. Both consumers and industrial buyers are unusually price-conscious in periods of recession, and consequently, price probably assumes a more important role in competitive strategy than it does in periods of economic normalcy or economic prosperity. Nevertheless, slightly more than one-half of the respondents did *not* select pricing as *one of the five* most important policy areas in their firm's marketing success. This is even more revealing when one notes that in the questionnaire the two major facets of nonprice competition were subdivided into a number of policy areas (e.g., sales effort was subdivided into sales research and sales planning, management of sales personnel, and advertising and sales promotions). In short, the competitive activities relating to the product and sales efforts were selected as most important in the success of these well-managed firms.[11]

---

[11] For more extensive analysis of the response, including analyses by major type of industry, see Jon G. Udell, *A Model of Non-Price Competitive Strategy* (Madison, Wisconsin: Bureau of Business Research and Service, School of Business, The University of Wisconsin, 1963).

While contrary to the visualization of business behavior suggested by microeconomic theory, the relative position of pricing does *not* imply that pricing is unimportant. Prices are still a major allocator of resources and determinant of success in the market place. However, from *management's* point of view, and perhaps the consumer's, pricing is less important than some other elements of competitive strategy. This conclusion is not surprising in light of the current economic and social environment of modern industry. Six factors may account for the perceived importance of the nonprice facets:

1. *The relatively well-to-do consumers of today are interested in more than just price.* They are interested in product quality, distinctiveness, style, and many other factors which lead to both physical and psychological satisfaction. Consumers not only can afford, but want product differentiation and sales promotion. From them the consumer receives a great deal of psychological satisfaction and utility. It is only logical that consumer-oriented managements would choose to emphasize product and sales efforts in an attempt to satisfy consumer desires.

2. The products of modern industry are fairly complex, and buyers often require a substantial amount of information in making purchase devisions. Marketing communications, in addition to being persuasive, are a major source of information about products, prices, and suppliers. Also important is the fact that many marketing communications help to reduce the amount of searching time required of buyers. Research has shown that buyers find it convenient to review advertisements at their leisure rather than to secure information by entering the market place to compare products and prices.[12] Therefore, the informative value of sales efforts is important to buyers and sellers alike.

3. In today's competitive economy, *supply*—or production capacity—*generally exceeds demand,* and, therefore, nearly all sellers are forced to be either highly competitive or almost collusive in

---

[12] Jon G. Udell, "Prepurchase Behavior of Buyers of Small Electrical Appliances," *Journal of Marketng,* XXX (October, 1966), pp. 50-52; and Bruce LeGrande and Jon G. Udell, "Consumer Behavior in the Market Place: An Empirical Study of Television and Furniture Purchasing with Theoretical Implications," *Journal of Retailing,* XL (Fall, 1964), pp. 32-40.

their pricing. Because there may be little or no freedom for a company to deviate from the market price, pricing sometimes is not a meaningful parameter of competitive strategy.

4. Most American manufacturing industries are oligopolistic; because of the small number of firms, the demand curves, prices, and sales of rival firms are highly interdependent. This makes it almost impossible to underprice competitors successfully if their products are similar and if there is excess capacity in the industry.[13] Because product differences and sales efforts are considerably more difficult to match than a reduction in price, rivals often resort to nonprice competitive tactics.

5. *It is through successful product differentiation that a manufacturer may obtain some pricing freedom.* Products known to be identical must be priced identically in the market place. However, if a product can be favorably differentiated in the eyes of the customer, some degree of pricing freedom is usually achieved.

6. The economic development of a nation and its industries is, to a considerable extent, dependent on the nonprice facets. As Walt Rostow has pointed out, the development, promotion, and distribution of new products provide people with an incentive to work and the desire to consume.[14] While investment and capital are often credited as being most important in economic development, it can be argued that marketing and consumption are equally important propellants of economic growth.

Implications For Theory

In today's economic and social setting it is not difficult to see why business management chooses to emphasize the nonprice facets of competitive behavior. This is not to imply that pricing is unimportant. However, the other facets of competition, given a reasonable level of prices, are often more important to both consumers and the firm. *If the theory of the firm is to be realistic*

---

[13] Paul M. Sweezy, "Demand Under Conditions of Oligopoly," *The Journal of Political Economy*, XLVII (1939), pp. 568-573.
[14] Walt W. Rostow, "The Concept of a National Market and Its Economic Growth Implications," *Proceedings of the American Marketing Association* (Fall, 1965), p. 19.

[35]

or useful, the role of nonprice competitive behavior must be adequately emphasized. The major purpose of an economic theory or economic model is to provide a simplified and workable representation of reality. This simplified representation is composed of the key economic and social variables that are at work in the economy. In developing a theory or model, the theorist strives to subjectively, graphically, or mathematically specify the relationships between the variables he has chosen. The purpose is usually twofold: to explain the real world and to predict. No theory or model of firm behavior can accomplish either of these objectives unless the role of nonprice competitive behavior receives adequate representation.

CHAPTER IV

PERCEIVED IMPORTANCE OF THE ELEMENTS OF STRATEGY

While *strategy* stems from the Greek word *strategia* meaning generalship, it is as suitable to business behavior as it is to military behavior. *Strategy is the science and art of manipulating available resources to accomplish desired objectives.* While the typical business firm may have several objectives, such as security, corporate growth, profits, and public service, a major objective of competitive or marketing strategy is sales. Sales, or the patronage of customers, are a necessary antecedent to accomplishing the goals of the firm. While other objectives are ultimately more important, without sales there can be no security, growth, profits, or service to society. However, the same can be said for profits —profits are a necessary prerequisite for remaining in business and, in some instances, the primary reason for being in business. Therefore, the major and most universal objectives of marketing strategy are sales and profits.

Because the firm is in competition with other businesses for the patronage of consumers (industrial, institutional, or ultimate consumers), marketing strategy—like military strategy— includes rivalry. While the intensity of the rivalry may vary dramatically from one industry to another, there is always some competition for the patronage of consumers. Most firms are in direct rivalry with other businesses, and *all* firms have indirect rivals. Even the publicly granted monopolies, such as electric utilities, have rivals from other industries. This rivalry extends beyond other producers of fuel and power. For example, in the all-electric home the consumer may conserve on the use of electricity in order to finance expenditures for food, clothing, sporting goods, or other desired products and services.

[37]

There apparently is little to be gained from distinguishing between the terms competitive strategy and marketing strategy.[1] Both involve some degree of rivalry with other firms and both pertain to the manipulation of available resources to profitably earn the patronage of consumers and accomplish the other objectives of the firm. Therefore, marketing strategy and competitive strategy may be used interchangeably and will be so used in the following pages for the sake of variety and to enhance the satisfaction of various readers who may prefer one term over another.

Competitive Strategy

The marketing strategy of a firm may be visualized or delineated in several ways. The simplest approach is to distinguish between price and nonprice competitive behavior. In the prior instance, the firm is in essence accepting its demand curve as given and manipulating its price in an attempt to attain objectives.[2]

When using nonprice strategy, the firm attempts to manipulate demand itself, i.e., to change the location and shape of its demand curve. The objective is to increase sales at any given price by shifting the demand curve to the right (as shown in Figure IV-1) or by decreasing the elasticity of demand (as shown in Figure IV-2).[3]

When elasticity of demand is decreased by nonprice efforts, the demand curve usually is shifted to the right as shown in Figure IV-2. However, the major impact of decreased elasticity is a decline in the responsiveness of demand to a change in price. This change enables the firm to raise price without much loss of sales. As a result, profits may rise as prices are raised because of the enlarged per unit revenue and because there is little reduction in the number of units sold. However, it usually is costly to shift or change the shape (elasticity) of the demand curve.

---

[1] However, this does not imply that the adjectives competitive and marketing, when used as nouns, are identical or similar in meaning.
[2] For oligopolistic industries, a single demand curve is an oversimplification. The more complex situation is presented in the chapter on pricing.
[3] Price elasticity is a measure of the responsiveness of demand to a change in price.

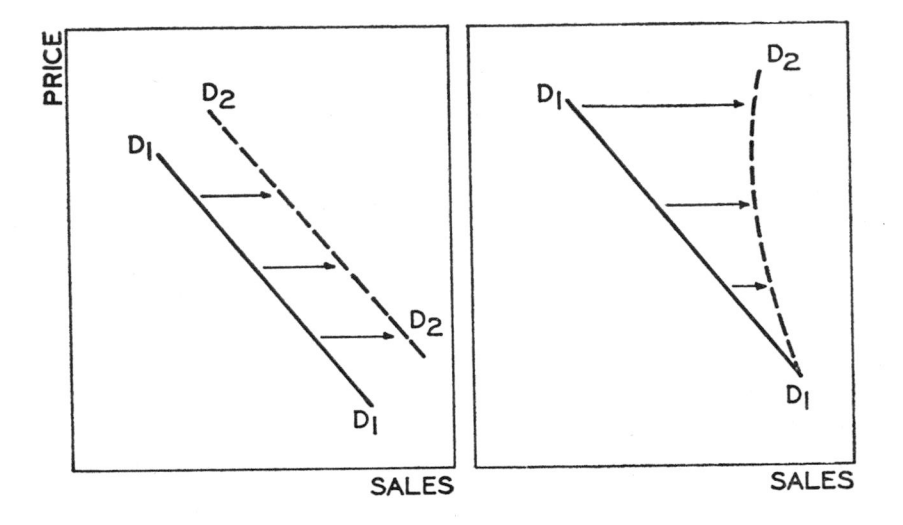

Figure IV–1
SHIFTING THE DEMAND
CURVE TO THE RIGHT

Figure IV–2
DECREASING THE
ELASTICITY OF DEMAND

D_1D_1 Demand curve before
nonprice strategy

D_2D_2 Demand curve as shifted
by nonprice strategy

D_1D_1 Demand curve before
nonprice strategy

D_2D_1 Demand curve as shifted
and made less elastic by
nonprice strategy

Management must determine whether the expanded revenues resulting from an enlarged demand and/or higher price are sufficient to more than offset the cost of the nonprice strategy necessary to produce the desired change in the demand curve.

As already indicated, a major purpose of this book is to provide a theoretical, but pragmatic, foundation for determining an optimum combination of the components of nonprice competitive strategy. The question of how much money and effort to invest in nonprice strategy will also be examined (see Appendix I).

Components of Nonprice Strategy

Nonprice strategy may be divided into two major facets— product effort and sales effort. Some prefer a threefold classification—product, promotion, and distribution. In the 1958 marketing management study, 11 categories of nonprice activities were delineated.

For purposes of developing a decision model for nonprice strategy, the two-way classification will be used—product effort and sales effort (including certain aspects of distribution). However, before presenting and testing that model, we shall evaluate two preliminary hypotheses by examining information pertaining to the competitive strategies for 485 apparently successful products:

> Hypothesis I — *The nonprice facets of competitive strategy are, from the manufacturer's point of view, at least as important as pricing.* Evidence has already been presented (the 1958 study) which supports this hypothesis. To further test the hypothesis, we shall examine more precise and recent information.
>
> Hypothesis II — *The importance of the nonprice facets will vary according to the behavioral characteristics of the market for a product and, to a more limited extent, the characteristics of the product itself.* For instance, the characteristics of the market for industrial goods vary considerably from those of the consumer nondurable goods market. If the second hypothesis is correct, the nonprice strategies for industrial goods, consumer dura-

bles, and consumer nondurables should differ significantly.[4]

While these hypotheses will be central to the development of a decision model for the prediction and management of nonprice strategy, the major purpose of the remainder of this chapter is to introduce data concerning the marketing strategies of U. S. manufacturers.

A Study Of Successful Products

With the support of the Graduate School of Business of The University of Wisconsin and the Graduate School of Business and Public Administration of Cornell University, and with the cooperation of hundreds of business executives, information on the competitive strategies for 485 specific products was gathered. Most of the executives participating in the study were either vice-presidents or general managers of their companies or their divisions of the companies. The respondents constituted 46 percent of the total mailing list. However, the response exceeded 50 percent of the excutives actually reached by the mail questionnaire survey.[5]

Methodology

The sample of apparently successful manufacturers was selected from *Fortune's Directory of 500 Largest Firms, Forbes' Seventeenth Annual Report on American Industry,* and *Poor's Register of Corporations, Directors, and Executives of the United States and Canada.* In selecting firms, emphasis was placed on profitability and the growth of sales and profits. An effort was made to include rapidly growing and profitable firms as well as large ones. However, most of the responses came from fairly large firms, as indicated by the fact that 65 percent of the products had sales volumes of $10 million or more. Forty-seven percent of the products enjoyed a market share of over 25 percent.[6]

---

[4] In forthcoming chapters, specific product and market characteristics will be identified and precise comparisons will be made.
[5] One thousand fifty-three chief executives of companies, or divisions of companies, constituted the total mailing list. However, because of deaths, transfers, and retirements, about 970 executives received the questionnaire.
[6] For a distribution of the sales volumes and market shares of the products included in the study, see Chapter IX.

The respondents were asked to select a product which is important to their company in terms of its contribution to total sales and profits. Because a product may sell to more than one market, and each market may require a separate marketing strategy, the executives were also asked to select a major market for their product.

Using a series of semantic differential questions (to be explained later), each respondent characterized the product and market he had chosen. He was then asked to estimate the relative importance of the competitive activities used in marketing the selected product. For each question, respondents allocated 100 points among the activities according to the estimated contribution of each to the success of the product. For example, the total marketing program was divided into four major facets:

> *Product Effort* — Includes product planning, product R & D, product testing, and the services accompanying the product.

> *Sales Effort* — Includes sales management and personal selling, advertising, and other marketing communications.

> *Distribution* — Includes the selection, development and evaluation of distribution channels, transportation, and inventory control.

> *Pricing Strategy* — Includes price determination and pricing policies.

In addition, each of the above facets was divided into five specific categories of competitive activities. Respondents were asked to allocate 100 points among the activities of each facet according to their relative importance in the success of the product. To insure that respondents clearly understood the scope of each major facet, the point allocations among the activities of each facet preceded the allocation of points among the four major facets. When the later allocation was made, each facet was again defined for the respondent. The high response rate and the lack of any indication of difficulty led the author to believe that the respondents did not have any problem determining what was meant by the various marketing terms used in the study.

IMPORTANCE OF STRATEGIC ELEMENTS

We now proceed to an overview of the research findings and a test of Hypothesis I—that nonprice facets are, from the manufacturer's point of view, at least as important as pricing.

Nonprice Strategy Most Important

As shown in Figure IV-3, business apparently disagrees with economic doctrine that the major facet of competitive behavior is pricing; the respondents, on the average, allocated only 18.4 out of 100 points to the pricing facet of competitive strategy.

Figure IV–3

PERCEIVED IMPORTANCE OF THE MAJOR FACETS OF MARKETING STRATEGY*

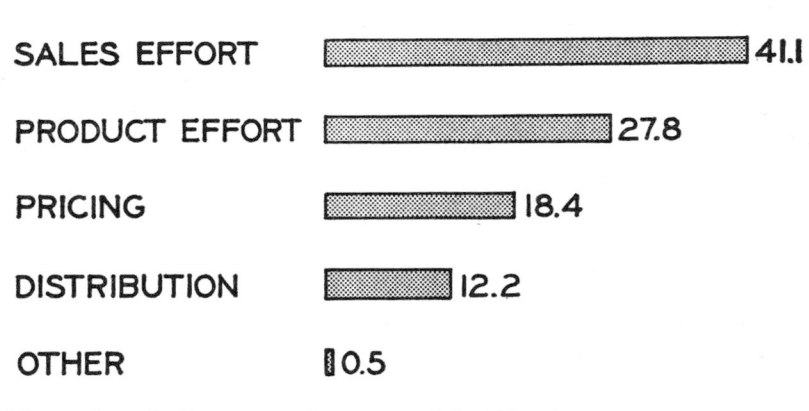

SALES EFFORT   41.1

PRODUCT EFFORT   27.8

PRICING   18.4

DISTRIBUTION   12.2

OTHER   0.5

*The total marketing strategy is represented by 100 points.

While a substantial misjudgment of the relative importance of any facet is possible, the fact remains that respondents allocated 81.6 points to the nonprice facets. Given the social and economic environment of American industry, management's perception of the relative importance of pricing in the success of a product is not unexpected. However, the perceived relative importance of pricing in no way implies that pricing strategy is unimportant, and pricing's relative importance to retailers and

wholesalers *may* be greater than it is to manufacturers.

The facet perceived to be most important in the marketing success of the selected products was sales effort or marketing communications—sales management, advertising, and other promotional programs. While this nonprice facet received, on the average, over 41 of the 100 points, product effort received about 28 points.

Sales effort is even more important than the 41 points suggest because the distribution facet included the selection and development of distribution channels. These are, to a great extent, sales effort activities. In using any channel other than producer-consumer, a manufacturer shifts part of his physical supply and sales effort responsibilities to the middlemen involved. Of the 12 points allocated to distribution, over one-half were for the determination, selection, and development of the channels of distribution. Therefore, *the average respondent attributed almost 50 percent of his product's success to the sales effort component of competitive strategy.*

As shown in Table IV-1, all types of producers—industrial, consumer durable, and consumer nondurable—selected sales effort as most important. (The only industries who ranked product effort over sales effort were producers of aerospace and defense equipment for the government.) Business evidently considers the creation of markets more important than the creation of products. In an economy where potential supply often exceeds effective demand, it is logical for management to emphasize the creation of markets.

Inasmuch as the creation of products is also considered highly important, the emphasis on sales effort is not inappropriate. As Joseph Schumpeter, the "father" of innovation theory, pointed out, invention alone does not foster economic growth or yield profits. It is through the implementation of an invention that progress and profits are achieved. For example, a developed but unpromoted and unmarketed cure for cancer would not contribute to the society's well-being. Likewise, a manufacturer cannot recover its R & D and production costs unless the product is successfully promoted and sold.

IMPORTANCE OF STRATEGIC ELEMENTS

Strategies Vary by Industry

One would not expect the marketing strategy of an electronic computer manufacturer to be similar to that of a cosmetic producer. Similar competitive conditions might induce like pricing practices, as economic theory suggests, but nonprice competitive strategies should vary according to the nature of the product and the behavioral characteristics of the market (Hypothesis II).

Without specifying exactly how the industrial, consumer durable, and consumer nondurable industries differ from one another, and how these differences should influence an optimum marketing strategy (topics to be covered in forthcoming chapters), Table IV-1 presents the perceived importance of the major facets of competitive strategy.

Table IV-1

PERCEIVED IMPORTANCE OF THE FACETS OF COMPETITIVE STRATEGY IN MAJOR INDUSTRIES*

Facet	Industrial Goods	Consumer Durables	Consumer Nondurables
Sales Effort	40.9	37.5	44.7
Distribution	10.1	18.7	16.3
Production Effort	29.6	24.3	22.8
Pricing	19.0	19.0	16.0
Other	.4	.5	.2
Total Strategy	100.0	100.0	100.0

*The data are the average point allocations of 344 industrial, 52 consumer durable, and 89 consumer nondurable goods manufacturers.

As shown, sales effort (marketing communications) was most important among manufacturers of consumer nondurables. If the definition of sales effort is expanded to include channel of distribution activities, one finds that over one-half (52.8 percent) of the total strategy points for consumer nondurables were allocated to marketing communications and channels of distribution. Consumer durable goods manufacturers allocated 49.4 percent of their points to these facets, while industrial goods producers allocated 45.2 percent.

[45]

SUCCESSFUL MARKETING STRATEGIES

The perceived importance of the product facet of competition also varied among the three industry groups. Industrial goods producers allocated 29.6 percent of their 100 points to product effort, while consumer durable manufacturers allocated 24.3 percent. Consumer nondurable goods producers allocated only 22.8 points to the product facet.

Sales Effort Strategies Differ

The general comparison of points allocated to the major facets of competition does not tell the whole story. The allocation of points to the specific components of product and sales effort differs markedly among the three major types of industries.

As previously mentioned, each of the major facets of competition was subdivided into five specific categories of activities. For example, the sales effort activities were sales management and personal selling, broadcast media advertising, printed media advertising, special promotional activities, branding and promotional packaging. Respondents allocated 100 points among these according to their perceived importance in the success of the product.

Sales management and personal selling was considered the most important type of marketing communication by all major types of manufacturers. As shown in Table IV-2, producers of industrial goods allocated 69 of their sales effort points to this activity, whereas consumer durable and nondurable goods producers allocated 48 and 38 points, respectively. This allocation, plus the fact that the sales effort facet received more points than any other major facet of competitive strategy, indicates that *sales management and personal selling is more important than any other specific marketing activity.* Support for this conclusion is provided by the marketing expenditures of U. S. industry. While reliable estimates for sales management and personal selling are not available, it is generally recognized that the expenditure involved greatly exceeds the amount spent on advertising, product development, or any other major category of marketing expenditures.

Advertising was the second most important sales effort activity of the producers of consumer nondurables; they allocated

an average of 36 percent of their sales effort points to television, radio, newspaper, magazine, and other printed media advertising.

Advertising was also the second most important activity in the marketing communications for consumer durable goods and industrial products. In total, consumer durable producers allocated 27 points to print and broadcast media advertising. While advertising was perceived as less important in the success of the industrial goods, print media advertising received an average of about 13 points and broadcast media received one point.

Special promotional activities such as trade shows, promotional warranties, and dealer aids were fairly important to all types of

Table IV-2

RELATIVE IMPORTANCE OF THE ELEMENTS OF MARKETING COMMUNICATIONS*

Sales Effort Activity	Producers of:		
	Industrial Goods	Consumer Durables	Consumer Nondurables
Sales Management & Personal Selling	69.2	47.6	38.1
Broadcast Media Advertising	.9	10.7	20.9
Printed Media Advertising	12.5	16.1	14.8
Special Promotional Activities	9.6	15.5	15.5
Branding & Promotional Packaging	4.5	9.5	9.8
Other	3.3	.6	.9
Total	100.0	100.0	100.0

*The data are the average point allocations of 336 industrial, 52 consumer durable, and 88 consumer nondurable goods producers. Nine responses are excluded because of point allocations which did not equal 100.

manufacturers. Industrial goods producers allocated 10 points to these promotions, whereas consumer goods producers allocated about 16 points.

Product branding and promotional packaging received 5 points from industrial goods producers and 10 points from consumer goods manufacturers.

SUCCESSFUL MARKETING STRATEGIES

The Varying Nature of Product Efforts

When the product facet was subdivided into five categories of activities, it was found that product service was much more important in the marketing of industrial goods than in the marketing of consumer goods. Presale service, such as product application engineering, and postsale service (including installation, maintenance, and warranty service) received 41 of the 100 points allocated by industrial goods manufacturers (see Table IV-3). Consumer durable and consumer nondurable goods producers allocated 27 and 21 points, respectively, to the two types of product service.

Table IV–3

RELATIVE IMPORTANCE OF THE ELEMENTS OF PRODUCT STRATEGY*

Product Effort Activity	Producers of:		
	Industrial Goods	Consumer Durables	Consumer Nondurables
Presale Service	23.7	12.8	12.1
Postsale Service	17.7	14.2	9.2
Technical R & D	34.5	34.6	38.6
Market Research	15.7	17.8	27.5
Style R & D	6.1	18.8	9.6
Other	2.3	1.9	3.0
Total	100.0	100.0	100.0

*Data are the average responses of 334 industrial, 52 consumer durable, and 87 consumer nondurable goods manufacturers. Eleven responses are excluded because of point allocations not equaling 100.

Because service was more important to industrial goods producers, they were left with fewer points to allocate among the various types of product research. However, technical R & D received about the same number of points from each type of manufacturer—around 35 points.

Marketing research concerning product planning and development and product testing received about 16 points from producers of industrial goods, 18 points from consumer durables, and 28 points from manufacturers of consumer nondurables. Apparently, marketing research is considerably more important to the latter group of producers.

[48]

IMPORTANCE OF STRATEGIC ELEMENTS

As to be expected, research relating to product styling and fashion was most important to producers of consumer durable goods. They allocated 19 points to this type of product research.

Considering the above and the fact that industrial goods manufacturers allocated the most points to the product facet of competition,[7] one finds that technical research and development, pre-sale service, and postsale service are more important in industrial goods marketing than in consumer goods marketing.

Distribution

The distribution facet of competition, as defined in the study, has two major components—physical supply and working with the channels of distribution. As indicated earlier, the selection and development of channels of distribution are, to a major extent, part of the sales facet of competitive strategy. Manufacturers utilizing middlemen transfer many of their selling activities to the channel of distribution, whereas those not utilizing middlemen must assume these activities.

Producers of consumer nondurable goods and industrial goods allocated 50 and 52 points respectively, to transportation, warehousing and inventory control (see Table IV-4). In contrast, consumer durable goods manufacturers allocated 35 points to the physical supply functions.

Consumer durable goods manufacturers allocated 63 points to the determination, selection, assistance, and development of channels of distribution. Industrial and consumer nondurable goods producers assigned 43 and 50 points, respectively, to these activities. In addition, the durable goods manufacturers allocated the most points to the overall distribution facet of competition.[8] Therefore, working with the channels of distribution is, by a substantial margin, most important to manufacturers of consumer durable goods.

---

[7] Industrial goods producers allocated 29.6 points to the overall product facet; while consumer durable and nondurable goods manufacturers allocated 24.3 and 22.8 points, respectively, to product effort.

[8] Consumer durable producers allocated 18.7 points to distribution, while consumer nondurable and industrial goods producers allocated 16.3 and 10.1 points, respectively.

Table IV–4

RELATIVE IMPORTANCE OF THE ELEMENTS OF DISTRIBUTION*

Distribution Activity	Producers of:		
	Industrial Goods	Consumer Durables	Consumer Nondurables
Transportation	23.8	12.2	26.8
Warehousing and Inventory Control	28.3	22.7	23.6
Determination of Channels	10.5	14.7	13.6
Selection of Establishments in Channels	13.3	21.7	14.6
Assistance to and Development of the Channel	19.1	27.0	21.4
Other	5.1	1.7	—
Total	100.0	100.0	100.0

*Data are the average point allocations of 298 industrial goods producers, 52 consumer durable, and 87 consumer nondurable goods manufacturers. Most of the aerospace and defense contractors had allocated very few points to the distribution facet and did not complete the distribution section of the questionnaire.

Limitations of the Data

A major disadvantage of using empirical data is that the research findings tend to describe *how* businesses compete, rather than *how they should* compete. To minimize this limitation, financial information was used to select a sample of apparently successful manufacturers. More important, each respondent was asked to choose a product and market which were successful in terms of their contribution to the sales and profit of the company. Obviously, all the products included in the study were not equally successful. Because of differences in corporate objectives, accounting procedures, market potentials and competitive conditions, the author could not conceive of any objective and universal standard for measuring success. Underlying this approach is the assumption that an established and successful product of a profitable company would have a marketing program which approaches an optimal strategy.

A second possible limitation is the fact that the data are *management's perceptions* of the relative importance of the various facets of competitive strategy. However, what alternatives are available? Expenditure data cannot be used because pricing

does not involve a direct expenditure, cost accounting systems vary from one company to another, and each facet undoubtedly has differing returns to scale (therefore, a comparison of the amounts spent on each facet could be misleading).

The opinions of someone other than management might be used to judge the relative contributions of various activities to the success of a product. However, it could be seriously questioned whether the perceptions of an outside analyst would be as accurate as those who have successfully managed the product.

Summary

All major facets of competitive strategy are essential to the successful marketing of a product. However, the nonprice facets were most important to each of the 485 manufacturers participating in the study.

The marketing strategies varied considerably from industry to industry. The product facet was most important among manufacturers of industrial goods and least important among producers of consumer nondurables. The sales effort facet, or marketing communications, was most important among companies marketing consumer nondurable goods. This finding remains firm when activities relating to the channels of distribution are considered as part of sales effort. The differences among the strategies of the major industries were large enough to suggest that a realistic and useful theory of marketing and competitive behavior might be based on the characteristics of a product's market.

The perceived importance of certain specific marketing activities in the success of the respondents' products is shown in Table IV-5. The most important competitive activity for all types of manufacturers was sales management and personal selling. Considering only the nonprice activities, product service and technical R & D were second and third in importance for industrial goods producers. Manufacturers of consumer durables rated distribution channels and advertising as second and third in importance. Advertising was almost as important as sales management among the consumer nondurable goods producers. These respondents rated technical R & D as third in importance; however, it was only slightly more important than the development of channels of distribution.

Table IV–5

IMPORTANCE OF SPECIFIC MARKETING ACTIVITIES
IN THE TOTAL COMPETITIVE STRATEGY*

Marketing Activity	Producers of:		
	Industrial Goods	Consumer Durables	Consumer Nondurables
Sales Management & Personal Selling	28.3	17.9	17.0
Advertising	5.5	10.1	16.0
Technical R & D	10.2	8.4	8.8
Selection and Development of Distribution Channels	4.3	11.9	8.1
Product Service	12.3	6.6	4.9
Pricing	19.0	19.0	16.0
All Other Competitive Activities	20.4	26.1	29.2
Total Strategy	100.0	100.0	100.0

*Data are averages calculated by multiplying the number of points allocated to the major facet times the number of points allocated to the activity which is part of that facet. The pricing facet is included as one activity; however, pricing was subdivided into five strategies in the research questionnaire.

If it is not subdivided into specific categories of activities, as were the other major facets of strategy,[9] pricing is visualized as second in importance to industrial goods manufacturers and first in importance to producers of consumer goods. However, the fact remains that management perceives the nonprice facets as substantially more important than pricing in the success of products.

[9] Perceptions concerning the role and importance of specific pricing policies will be presented in Chapter VIII.

CHAPTER V

A DECISION MODEL FOR NONPRICE STRATEGY

In the past few decades, a number of nonprice variables have been added to the classical and neoclassical theories of firm behavior. As previously mentioned, Edward Chamberlin introduced product differentiation and the monopolistically competitive market structure. Joe S. Bain presented the concept of limit pricing and the condition of entry. William Fellner emphasized the roles of uncertainty and firm recognition of interdependence. The works of these and other economists are significant contributions, but they fall short of providing an adequate theory of nonprice competitive strategy. With only a few exceptions, these theoretical developments have one thing in common—they relate firm behavior to the market structure of the industry. Certainly the behavior of a firm may be influenced by the size and number of its competitors, the degree of recognition of interdependence, and the amount of collusion among the competitors. Bringing these factors into the theory of firm behavior is necessary, but these factors alone do not explain *how* a firm will compete (or should compete) for the consumer's dollar.

It has been suggested that the importance of the facets of nonprice strategy will vary according to the behavioral characteristics of the market for a product and, to a more limited extent, the characteristics of the product itself. The producer of newsprint does not use the same marketing strategy as a manufacturer of cigarettes. A comparison of the structures of the newsprint and cigarette industries would not explain the differences between their marketing strategies. For this reason, it is suggested that the product-market be incorporated into the theories and models of competitive behavior.

[53]

Product-Market Characteristics

The product-market—the nature of a product in relation to the behavioral characteristics of the buyers and potential buyers for the product—may be delineated by four interrelated variables.

1. Knowledge of the Buyer
2. Effort of the Buyer
3. Purchaser's Buying Motives
4. Technical Nature of the Product

Knowledge of the Buyer

Knowledge of the buyer is defined as the level of comprehension and understanding that the purchaser has in regard to the product and particularly its want-satisfying power. This would include the buyer's comprehension of the product's composition, operation, and application. However, as the definition implies, primary emphasis is placed upon the buyer's knowledge of the ability of the product to satisfy his wants and needs (physical and psychological). Knowledge of a product's composition, operation, and application is necessary only to the extent that it aids the buyer in judging the product's utility to him.

While buyers' knowledge concerning a product is never perfect, it can vary dramatically among products, markets, and individual purchasers. For example, the purchasing agent for an electrical utility will have far greater information concerning the properties of various fuels than the typical consumer who purchases fuel to heat his home.

It is suggested that the extent or degree of buyers' knowledge will affect the optimum nonprice strategy of the firm. More specifically, the importance of product effort should vary directly with knowledge, while the importance of sales effort should vary inversely with the knowledge of the purchaser. Obviously, if buyers have a high level of comprehension and understanding concerning a product, they do not need the information conveyed by marketing communications. In addition, the buyers' opinions concerning the product will be based on their knowledge and are not likely to be swayed by the persuasions of the manufacturer. In this instance, the manufacturer must emphasize the quality

[54]

of his product and service, rather than marketing communications.

Contrary to classical competitive theory, the knowledge of the buyer is usually imperfect. Therefore, one would expect marketing communications to be important in most industries, and most important in those where the buyers' knowledge is least.

Effort of the Buyer

Effort of the buyer is defined as the amount of time, expense, and consideration which the typical purchaser puts forth to acquire a given product. For example, when Mr. Jones desires a package of cigarettes, he is not willing to put forth a great amount of effort to obtain a specific brand or to buy from a specific vendor. He usually will make his purchase at the most convenient retail outlet. This is true, by definition, of all convenience goods.[1]

On the other hand, when Mr. Jones decides to purchase a new automobile, he is willing to put forth a substantial amount of time, expense and consideration in the effort to obtain an automobile which, for the price paid, best meets his needs and desires. This is true, to a greater or lesser extent, of most shopping goods[2] and specialty goods.[3] It is even more true of industrial goods[4] where the time and effort of several corporate executives may be involved in a purchase transaction.

Buyers devote time, expense, and consideration in an attempt to optimize the satisfaction they receive from their purchases. In economic terminology, the marginal utility received from the last unit of effort devoted to making the purchase should equal the marginal disutility or cost of that last unit of effort. Buyers will not devote much time and expense to the purchase of those products where the utility resulting from additional effort is low. This is true of most inexpensive convenience goods such as bread and razor blades. On the other hand, the marginal return to

---

[1] Convenience goods may be defined as those which consumers wish to purchase rapidly and with a minimum of time and effort.

[2] Shopping goods are those goods which are usually purchased after the consumer has compared quality, price, and style.

[3] Specialty goods are defined as those goods which consumers characteristically insist upon and for which they are willing to make a special purchase effort.

[4] Industrial goods are those goods consumed in the production of goods (and services) or in operating an institution.

[55]

buyers' effort can be substantial in the case of higher-priced goods and services.

Buyers who invest substantial effort in making a purchase are likely, other factors being equal, to make a careful and accurate evaluation of alternative products and brands. Therefore, the importance of the product facet should vary directly with the effort of the buyer. On the other hand, the importance of sales effort should tend to vary inversely with buyer effort. Highly promoted products tend to be quickly accepted when buyer effort is minimal.

Purchaser's Buying Motives

Product buying motives are the impulses, desires, and other considerations of the buyer which induce the purchase of certain goods and services. They are the drives that prompt the sequence of activities known as purchasing behavior.[5] All goods are purchased for their estimated utility (i.e., the buyers' estimation of their capacity to yield personal satisfaction) or their productivity—their capacity to help produce a product or service efficiently.

Purchaser's buying motives may be classified as operational and socio-psychological.[6] Operational buying motives are those directly related to the anticipated performance of the product. Their satisfaction is derived from the physical performance of the product. The majority of product buying motives for industrial goods are of this type. For example, a road construction company purchases a new dump truck because it will serve the firm by hauling construction materials. A consumer's operational buying motive is illustrated by a homeowner's purchase of an efficient oil burner to heat his home.

Socio-psychological buying motives are those which are indirectly related to the anticipated performance of the product and directly related to the purchaser's social and psychological interpretation of the product. The primary source of utility is the psychological satisfaction received from the ownership, use

---

[5] For a more complete discussion of buying motives, see Jon G. Udell, "A New Approach to Consumer Motivation," *Journal of Retailing*, XL, (Winter, 1964-65), pp. 6-10.
[6] *Ibid.*, p. 9.

and social prestige of the product. This psychic utility is, at most, indirectly derived from the product's performance. Furthermore, the psychological satisfaction may be received at the buyer's conscious or subconscious level of thought. If a young lady received psychic utility from a bottle of Chanel No. 5 perfume because a beautiful girl embraced by a handsome gentleman was pictured in an advertisement for the perfume, she probably is receiving psychological satisfaction at a subconscious level. However, if the satisfaction is primarily derived from her recognition of the social prestige of Chanel No. 5, she is receiving utility at the more conscious level.

As shown in Figure V-1, the potential source of satisfaction is the controlling factor in distinguishing between the two types of buying motives. However, rarely is a product purchased on the basis of one motive, and the motives inducing a purchase are seldom entirely operational or socio-psychological. Therefore, the motives inducing the purchase of a product should be visualized as existing on a continuum between the two extremes.

Figure V-1
PRODUCT BUYING MOTIVE CONTINUUM

Operational Buying Motives	Socio-Psychological Buying Motives
Satisfaction to be derived from physical performance of the product.	Satisfaction to be derived from consumer's social and psychological interpretation of the product and its performance.

Because operational buying motives are satisfied by actual product performance, the product facet should be most important where operational buying motives are predominant. Where socio-psychological buying motives are predominant, sales effort should be especially important because marketing communications can help to create a favorable image or psychological interpretation of the product; this image is a major element in the satisfaction of the socio-psychological motives which prompted the purchase.

Technical Nature of the Product

Technical nature of the product is defined as the complexity of a commodity from the point of view of its user. In the case of a homemaker buying wrapping paper for mailing packages and other household uses, paper would be considered a relatively nontechnical product. She would not be concerned about the intricate complexities of various paper compositions, nor would she need any special technical information to use the paper. However, paper would be considered a technical product by the General Electric Company when it purchases special paper to use in the insulation of electrical transformers. Therefore, as it affects competitive strategy, the technical nature of the product is measured from the point of view of the market to whom the product is to appeal. If the product is highly technical, one would expect product quality (and product service) to be of major importance in the marketing strategy of the manufacturer. Conversely, if the product is substantially less technical, sales efforts are likely to be of greater relative importance.

This, of course, does not preclude sales effort from being highly important in the sale of a complex product if *other* factors, such as the customers' need for information about the product, indicate extensive sales effort. In other words, all characteristics of the product-market may not indicate the same marketing strategy.

Undoubtedly, there are other behavioral and product variables which exert a strong influence on an optimum, nonprice competitive strategy, and the above may not constitute the best combination of variables. However, the identification and testing of other variables should come after the original variables have been evaluated.

The Product-Market Model

With four attributes of product-market defined,[7] two inversely related hypotheses concerning the nonprice competitive strategy of the firm are proposed:

---

[7] At an earlier date, five variables were used to define the product-market. The fifth—value of typical purchase—was intercorrelated with the other four variables and has been dropped.

A DECISION MODEL FOR NONPRICE STRATEGY

1. The importance of the product facet of competitive behavior varies directly with the effort of the buyer, the technical nature of the product, the knowledge of the buyer, and the importance of operational buying motives. In other words, the greater the purchasing effort of the buyer, the more technical the product, the greater the knowledge of the buyer, and the more important the operational buying motive—the more important will be the product facet of nonprice competition.

2. The importance of the sales effort facet of competitive activity varies inversely with the efforts of the buyer, the technical nature of the product and the knowledge of the buyer, while varying directly with the importance of socio-psychological buying motives. In short, the importance of sales effort tends to be associated with the lack of purchasing effort by the buyer, less technical products, a low level of buyer knowledge, and the predominance of socio-psychological buying motives.

Symbolically, the hypotheses may be expressed by the following equations:

$$(1) \quad PE = a_0 + a_1 E^{n_1} + a_2 T^{n_2} + a_3 K^{n_3} + a_4 O^{n_4}$$

$$(2) \quad SE = b_0 - b_1 E^{m_1} - b_2 T^{m_2} - b_3 K^{m_3} + b_4 S^{m_4}$$

where a_i, $b_j \geq 0$; i, $j \geq 1$ and:

PE = Importance of Product Effort
SE = Importance of Sales Effort
E = Effort of the Buyer
T = Technical Nature of the Product
K = Knowledge of the Buyer
O = Strength of the Operational Buying Motives
S = Strength of Socio-Psychological Buying Motives

[59]

As the equations suggest, the importance of sales effort and the importance of product effort are determined by the combined effect of the values of all the attributes. However, for purposes of practical analysis, it is convenient to measure each attribute and then estimate the combined effect of all attributes. The role played by each attribute is not necessarily 25 percent of the total importance of the four variables. In practice, the relative importance of each variable would be estimated on the basis of past experience, research, and management intuition. Also, it is possible for the value and importance of a variable to change. For example, in recent years the automobile has declined in importance as a status symbol. A considerable portion of the social prestige which once accompanied the ownership of a large, powerful and expensive automobile has been transferred to other products, such as boats and homes. As a result, the socio-psychological buying motive, although still significant, probably does not play as important a role in automobile purchasing as it once did.

A second major point concerning the two hypotheses is that the importance of one facet of nonprice competitive strategy does not preclude the coexisting importance of the other. The value of some of the product-market attributes may favor a product-oriented strategy, while other attributes favor sales effort. Also, the predominance of one type of buying motive does not preclude the importance of the other type of buying motive. The buying motives prompting the purchase of automobiles illustrate this point. Performance, reliability, economy, safety and other operational motives may be the most important in the purchase of an automobile. However, this does not prevent the desire for style, luxury, prestige, and other socio-psychological factors from strongly entering into the purchasing decision. In short, the sum of the attributes for each product-market is different.

In light of the above, it is obvious that the model is not, from a theoretical point of view, as rigorous as one might desire. The exact importance of each attribute cannot be judged "a priori," and the resulting importance of the two facets of nonprice competition cannot be precisely determined. However, the model may provide a pragmatic theoretical approach for explaining and predicting the optimum nonprice strategy of the firm. Hav-

ing obtained measurements (or estimates) of the value and importance of each of the product-market attributes, and having evaluated their combined influence, management can roughly determine the optimum balance of product effort and sales effort to use in the marketing strategy for a product.

Evaluation Of The Model

Because the data to be used in testing the model are based on perceptions of the relative importance of the various facets of competitive strategy, the hypotheses of the model should be restated accordingly:

1. The relative importance of sales effort should vary directly with the strength of socio-psychological buying motives, while varying inversely with the purchasing efforts and knowledge of the buyer and the technical nature of the product.

2. The relative importance of product effort should vary directly with the strength of operational buying motives, the purchasing efforts and the knowledge of the buyer, and the technical nature of the product.

The acceptance or rejection of these hypotheses would also lead to the acceptance or rejection of the original model.

Measurement of the Product-Market

Measurements of each attribute of the product-market were obtained by using a five-point semantic-differential scale. For example, respondents were asked: "What is the effort of the buyer—the amount of time, expense, and consideration which the typical consumer puts forth in purchasing the product?" This category would include searching for alternative sources of supply, seeking specific brands, obtaining price information, and evaluating technical aspects of the product in relation to the use to which the product will be put.

1	2	3	4	5
Great Effort		Moderate Effort		Little or No Effort

Similar questions were asked to obtain a scale value for knowledge of the buyer, level of buyer comprehension, and the nature of the buying motives.

Sophisticated Product-Markets

A sophisticated product-market shall be defined as one where:
1. Buyer knowledge concerning the product and its want-satisfying power is great (a scale value of one on a scale running from one to five).
2. Buyer effort to make a wise purchase is substantial (a scale value of one).
3. Motives for purchasing the product are operational rather than socio-psychological in nature (a scale value of one—scale values approaching five denote increasing degrees of socio-psychological motivation).
4. Complexity of the product, from the purchasers' point of view, is substantial (a scale value of one).

Given this definition, a perfectly sophisticated market would have a total product-market profile of four and an average profile of one. Because the rating scales used in the study ranged from one to five, a perfectly unsophisticated market would have an average product-market profile of five.

For the purpose of evaluation, the product-market hypotheses may be restated in an abbreviated form: the importance of product effort varies directly with the sophistication of the product-market, while the importance of sales effort varies inversely with the degree of sophistication.

To test the hypotheses, the arithmetic mean and standard error of the differences between the means were calculated for the point allocations associated with each level of each product-market attribute. In addition, analysis of variance tests were made to evaluate the differences among groups of means.

The Product Effort Hypothesis

The average importance of product effort for each level of each product-market attribute is pictured graphically in Figure V-2. As shown, the importance of product effort in the firms' competitive strategies varied directly with the sophistication of the product-market (level one being most sophisticated, level

[62]

Figure V–2
**PERCEIVED IMPORTANCE OF PRODUCT EFFORT AND LEVELS OF
THE PRODUCT-MARKET ATTRIBUTES**

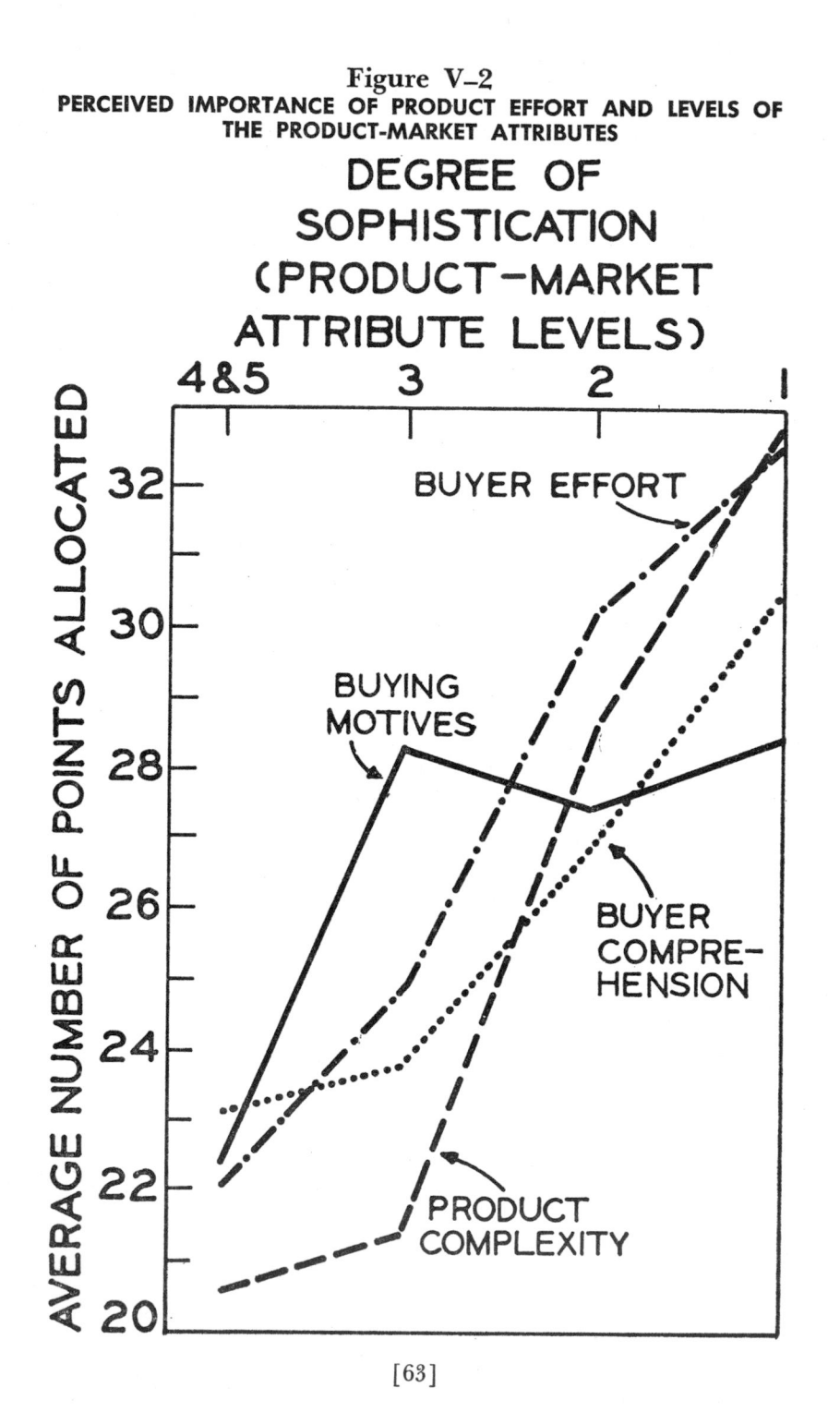

DEGREE OF
SOPHISTICATION
(PRODUCT—MARKET
ATTRIBUTE LEVELS)

five being least sophisticated). In presenting the means, levels four and five were combined because of the small number of respondents in these two groups.

The average number of points allocated to product effort is shown in Table V-1, together with the number of observations associated with each mean. For example, those respondents rating their products as highly complex (level one) allocated, on the average, 32.8 percent of their total competitive strategy to product effort. Those rating the complexity of their product as either four or five allocated an average of 20.6 points to product effort. Therefore, the results definitely indicate that the importance of product effort varies directly with the complexity of the product. The differences among the means of the four levels are statistically significant at the .01 level.[8]

In every instance except one, the average perceived importance of product effort declined as the attribute levels moved from one to five. The one exception was the 28.2 points allocated to level three of buying motives. This average was slightly higher than the 27.5 points allocated to level two of that attribute. The difference, however, was not statistically significant.

Even with the one exception, the overall allocation of points to product effort, classified according to the nature of the buying

Table V–1
AVERAGE POINT ALLOCATIONS TO PRODUCT EFFORT CLASSIFIED ACCORDING TO PRODUCT-MARKET ATTRIBUTE LEVELS

Product-Market Attributes	Product-Market Attribute Levels				
	1	2	3	4 & 5	F**
Product Complexity	32.8	28.5	21.5	20.6	13.338
(N*)	(202)	(122)	(91)	(65)	
Buying Motives	28.4	27.5	28.2	22.4	1.103
(N*)	(335)	(81)	(40)	(24)	
Buyer Effort	32.7	30.2	24.7	22.0	9.098
(N*)	(146)	(118)	(118)	(97)	
Buyer Comprehension	30.5	26.9	23.7	23.1	4.305
(N*)	(256)	(99)	(96)	(29.0)	

*N is the number of observations for each level of the product-market attributes.

**F values of 2.39 or larger are statistically significant at the .05 level; those that are 3.35 and larger are significant at the .01 level. The F values apply to the differences among the means.

[8] The relatively high concentration of observations in level one tends to reduce the statistical significance of the differences among the means. If the number of observations for each level were more equally distributed, a greater degree of statistical significance would result.

motives, supports the hypothesis that the importance of product effort varies directly with the predominance of operational buying motives. However, analysis of variance indicates that the differences among the means of the four levels are not statistically significant (when a five percent test is used). This may be due to the fact that most of the respondents (335) rated their customers' buying motives as completely operational. A more even distribution of respondents among the levels of this attribute would have produced a different result. Also, the buying motive rating of *some* of the respondents constitutes the most questionable aspect of the questionnaire results. For example, given the success of white sidewall tires and other appearance features, and the emotional advertising appeals frequently employed by tire manufacturers, it is somewhat difficult to accept a rating which implies that tire buyers are prompted exclusively by operational buying motives. However, *some* tire manufacturers selected a buying motive scale value of one.

Accepting the rating as received, one would conclude that the importance of product effort tends to vary directly with the predominance of operational buying motives, even though there is one exception and the results are not highly statistically significant. In this regard, note that level one had an average product effort point allocation of 28.4, while levels four and five had an average of 22.4.

The hypothesis that the extent of buyer effort and the importance of product strategy are directly related is supported by the average point allocations. For example, those with a buyer effort level of one allocated 32.7 points to product effort, as opposed to the 22.0 points allocated by those with a buyer effort level of four or five. The differences among the mean allocations are statistically significant at the .01 level.

The importance of product effort is also directly related to the level of buyer comprehension concerning the product and its want satisfying power. The differences among the means are significant at the .01 level.

In summary, the overall hypothesis is supported. *The importance of product effort in the competitive strategies of the American manufacturers was directly related to the level of buyer comprehension, buyer effort, product complexity, and the*

predominance of operational buying motives. The above tests are highly strenuous in that the average point allocations to product effort are based on many factors, not just the single attribute being tested. For example, a given manufacturer might have a complex product (such as a prescription drug) which is purchased for both operational and socio-psychological reasons, and without extensive buying effort and great buyer comprehension. In a situation such as this, it is difficult for product complexity, considered alone, to be directly related to the importance of product effort. Despite this difficulty, 15 of the 16 means (four levels of four attributes) support the product effort hypothesis.

The Sales Effort Hypothesis

The sales effort hypothesis was tested in a similar manner. As shown in Figure V-3 and Table V-2, the perceived importance of sales effort varies inversely with the sophistication of the product-market. In all but two of the 16 attribute level groups, the differences among means support the hypothesis.

Table V–2

AVERAGE POINT ALLOCATIONS TO SALES EFFORT CLASSIFIED ACCORDING TO PRODUCT-MARKET ATTRIBUTE LEVELS

Product-Market Attributes	Product-Market Attribute Levels				
	1	2	3	4 & 5	F**
Product Complexity	47.2	52.4	60.8	62.4	16.604
(N*)	(202)	(122)	(91)	(65)	
Buying Motives	52.1	54.3	52.9	64.4	3.042
(N*)	(335)	(81)	(40)	(24)	
Buyer Effort	46.5	51.1	56.6	61.5	13.521
(N*)	(146)	(118)	(118)	(97)	
Buyer Comprehension	49.7	55.8	58.8	56.1	6.091
(N*)	(256)	(99)	(96)	(29)	

*N is the number of observations for each level of the product-market attributes.
**F values of 2.39 or larger are statistically significant at the .05 level; those that are 3.35 and larger are significant at the .01 level. The F values apply to the differences among the means.

Looking first at product complexity, we find those respondents with highly complex products allocated an average of 47.2 points to sales effort, while those with the least complex products al-

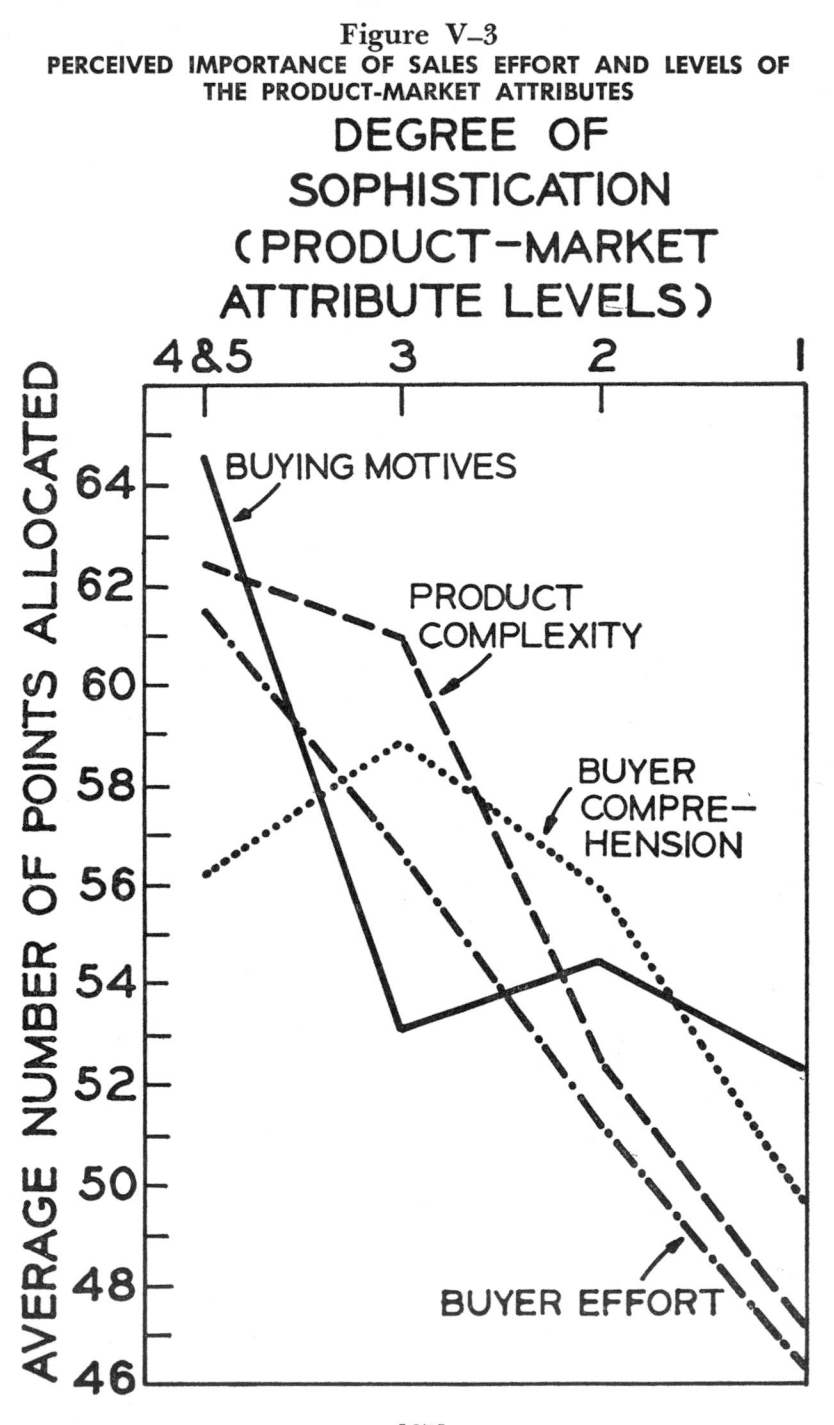

Figure V–3
PERCEIVED IMPORTANCE OF SALES EFFORT AND LEVELS OF
THE PRODUCT-MARKET ATTRIBUTES

DEGREE OF
SOPHISTICATION
(PRODUCT–MARKET
ATTRIBUTE LEVELS)

located 62.4 points. The differences among the means of the four groups is significant at the .01 level.

As in the case of product effort, the average number of sales effort points allocated at level three of buying motives deviates from the overall pattern and the hypothesis. However, those with predominately operational buying motives allocated significantly fewer points to sales effort than those with predominately socio-psychological buying motives. While the evidence is somewhat weak, the hypothesis is generally supported that sales effort is most important when buyers are prompted primarily by socio-psychological rather than operational buying motives. The differences among the means are statistically significant at the .05 level.

The hypothesis that the importance of sales effort varies inversely with the extent of buyer effort was vividly supported with means of 46.5, 51.1, 56.6, and 61.5 for levels one, two, three and four-five, respectively. The differences among the means are statistically significant at the .01 level.

The average importance of sales effort varied from 49.7 for level one to 56.1 for levels four and five of buyer comprehension. However, level three had the highest average. Using a one percent test, the differences among the means are statistically significant.

Therefore, with only two minor exceptions, the means provide definite and statistically significant support for the overall hypothesis that the importance of sales efforts will vary directly with the strength of socio-psychological buying motives and inversely with buyer effort, product complexity, and buyer comprehension.

Conclusion

In summary, the components of the deductively derived product-market hypotheses have been inductively (empirically) supported.

An overall test of the product effort and sales effort hypotheses is also possible, using the sum of the scale values. For example, those rating each attribute of the product-market as one would have a total scale value of four—the most sophisticated product-market possible. Those with highly sophisticated product-markets (sums of four, five, and six) allocated an average of 32.4

points to product effort. Those with the least sophisticated product-markets (sums of 16 through 20) allocated an average of only 18.0 points to product effort.

These same manufacturers allocated an average of 72.5 points to sales effort and distribution, while those with a highly sophisticated product-market allocated only 47.4 points to sales and distribution. Rather than present detailed information on these allocations, it is perhaps more useful to look at the allocations of specific industrial and consumer goods industries. This is done in the following two chapters and may constitute the most useful part of this book for the executive reader who must make decisions concerning the marketing mix and competitive strategy of his company.

CHAPTER VI

MARKETING STRATEGIES FOR
INDUSTRIAL GOODS

A general picture of the marketing strategies of industrial goods manufacturers was presented in Chapter III. However, the strategies used by the industrial producers varied considerably from one industry to another. In this chapter we will examine the product, sales, distribution, and pricing strategies of four industries: capital goods, industrial chemicals, fabricated parts and materials, and aerospace and defense. Because of the apparent importance of the product-market, we will look first at how the responding executives characterized the markets for their products.

Nature Of Industrial Markets

As previously defined, a sophisticated product-market is one where:

1. Buyer knowledge concerning the product and its want-satisfying power is great (a scale value of 1).
2. Buyer effort to make a wise purchase is substantial (a scale value of 1).
3. Motives for purchasing the product are operational rather than socio-psychological in nature (a scale value of 1).
4. Complexity of the product, from the purchasers' point of view, is substantial (a scale value of 1).

The average of the scale values selected by each respondent (i.e., the sum of the scale values divided by the number of attributes) shall be called the *average profile*. Therefore, the

most sophisticated product-market possible has an average profile of one; the least sophisticated product-market possible has an average profile of five.

As shown in Table VI-1, each of the four types of industrial goods producers has a relatively sophisticated product-market. The aerospace and defense industry has the most sophisticated market with an average profile of 1.2. The fabricated parts and materials industry has the least sophisticated product-market with an average profile of 1.9.

Table VI–1

PRODUCT-MARKET PROFILES FOR INDUSTRIAL GOODS INDUSTRIES*

	Average Profile	Buyer Knowledge	Buyer Effort	Purchase Motives	Product Complexity
Aerospace & Defense	1.2	1.3	1.3	1.1	1.1
Capital Goods	1.5	1.5	1.8	1.3	1.6
Industrial Chemicals	1.6	1.5	2.0	1.1	1.7
Fabricated Parts & Materials	1.9	1.7	2.3	1.3	2.0

*Profiles are based on the responses of 29 aerospace and defense contractors, 127 capital goods producers, 41 manufacturers of industrial chemicals, and 140 producers of fabricated parts and materials.

The Marketing Strategies

Producers of aerospace and defense equipment placed more emphasis on the product and pricing facets of competition and less emphasis on the sales effort and distribution facets than any other type of industrial goods producer. Given the sophisticated product-markets of the aerospace and defense industry and the hypotheses relating to the relative importance of product and sales efforts, the emphasis on product effort (and the relative lack of emphasis on sales effort) is to be expected.

According to the average product-market profiles of the four industries, product effort should be most important in the strategies of aerospace and defense contractors, next most important to capital goods producers, third most important to industrial chemical manufacturers, and least important to manufacturers of fabricated parts and materials. As shown in Table VI-2, the points allocated to the product effort facet conform to this expectation. Aerospace and defense producers allocated 50 percent

of their competitive strategy points to product effort, while manufacturers of fabricated parts and materials allocated only 25 points to this facet.

The perceived importance of both sales effort and distribution conforms to the hypothesis that the relative importance of sales effort will vary inversely with the sophistication of the product-market. More specifically, the importance of sales effort varied inversely with buyer knowledge, buyer purchasing effort, and complexity of the product while varying directly with the importance of socio-psychological motives prompting the purchase of the product.[1]

As anticipated by the hypothesis and the product-market profiles, sales effort is perceived as most important in the marketing of fabricated parts and materials (46 points), next most important in the marketing of industrial chemicals (42 points), and least important in the marketing strategies of aerospace and defense contractors (26 points). It is interesting to note that sales effort is perceived as the most important aspect of marketing by all types of producers, except those marketing aerospace and defense equipment to the federal government.

Pricing was about equally important to all types of industrial goods producers. However, it was, by a small margin, most important to aerospace and defense contractors.

Table VI–2

PERCEIVED IMPORTANCE OF THE MAJOR FACETS OF COMPETITIVE STRATEGY

Major Facet	Aerospace and Defense	Capital Goods	Industrial Chemicals	Fabricated Parts and Materials
Product Effort	49.9	30.9	26.9	25.0
Sales Effort	26.2	38.7	42.3	45.5
Distribution	1.5	10.5	11.1	11.3
Pricing	21.6	19.1	19.6	18.3
Other	.9	.7	.0	.0
Total Competitive Strategy*	100.0	100.0	100.0	100.0

*Totals do not exactly equal 100.0 because of rounding of the individual values.

[1] The 16 measures of the individual attribute values support this conclusion with one exception, the buying motives for industrial chemicals.

We will now turn to the more specific elements of the competitive strategies used by industrial goods producers.

Product Strategies

Aerospace and defense contractors (Table VI-3) allocated about one-half of their total product effort to the technical research and development of products. Another 33 points were allocated to presale and postsale service; market research received most of the remaining points.

Table VI–3

RELATIVE IMPORTANCE OF THE ELEMENTS OF PRODUCT STRATEGY

Product Effort Activity	Aerospace and Defense	Capital Goods	Industrial Chemicals	Fabricated Parts and Materials
Presale Service	20.0	23.7	18.6	25.9
Postsale Service	12.6	19.8	17.6	16.9
Technical R&D	49.3	33.0	33.9	32.9
Market Research	13.8	15.2	21.0	14.9
Style R&D	4.3	6.5	5.5	6.3
Other Product Effort	.0	1.8	3.4	3.0
Total Product Strategy	100.0	100.0	100.0	100.0

The product strategies of manufacturers selling to private industrial markets were fairly similar. All three classifications of producers attributed one-third of their product effort to technical R & D and 6 percent to style R & D. Product service was considered more important in the success of these producers than was technical R & D. Presale product service, such as application engineering, was most important to manufacturers of fabricated parts and materials and least important to producers of industrial chemicals. Postsale service, such as product installation, maintenance, and guarantee service, was most important to capital goods producers.

Market research relating to product planning and development received an average of 21 points from the industrial chemical producers and 15 points from the manufacturers of capital goods and fabricated parts.

In summary, there appears to be little difference in the product strategies of various types of firms selling to private indus-

trial markets. However, total product strategy is more important to capital goods producers than it is to manufacturers of industrial chemicals and fabricated parts and materials, and most important in the marketing efforts of the aerospace and defense industries.

Marketing Communications

Sales management and personal selling are, by a substantial margin, the most important sales effort activity of industrial goods manufacturers (Table VI-4). The average number of points allocated to sales management and personal selling ranged from 65 to 78. Capital goods producers allotted it the fewest points, whereas manufacturers of industrial chemicals gave sales management and personal selling the most emphasis.

Table VI–4

RELATIVE IMPORTANCE OF VARIOUS MARKETING COMMUNICATIONS

Sales Effort Activity	Aerospace & Defense	Capital Goods	Industrial Chemicals	Fabricated Parts & Materials
Sales Management and Personal Selling	74.7	65.3	77.7	69.2
Printed Media Advertising	10.8	14.6	10.5	11.6
Broadcast Media Advertising	.5	.9	.1	1.1
Special Promotional Activities	8.3	11.8	4.4	9.3
Branding & Promotional Packaging	1.7	4.4	4.0	5.4
Other Sales Efforts	4.0	3.0	3.2	3.4
Total Sales Effort	100.0	100.0	100.0	100.0

Printed media advertising was the second most important sales effort activity for each of the four industrial goods industries. The points allocated to printed media advertising ranged from about 11 among producers of industrial chemicals and aerospace and defense contractors to 15 for manufacturers of capital goods. Broadcast media advertising was of little importance to the industrial goods manufacturers. All advertising received the greatest emphasis among capital goods producers and the least

emphasis among aerospace and defense contractors.

Special promotional activities, such as trade shows, dealer aids, and promotional warranties were perceived to be the third most important sales effort activity for each of the industrial goods industries. However, the perceived importance varied considerably. Manufacturers of industrial chemicals allocated only four points to special promotional activities, while capital goods producers allocated 12 points to this element of sales effort.

Branding and promotional packaging was least in importance, receiving five points or less from each type of industrial goods manufacturer. Branding and packaging was most important to producers of fabricated parts and materials.

In summary, the sales effort strategies of the four types of industrial goods producers do not differ greatly. Each group of manufacturers attributes substantial importance to sales management and personal selling. It should be recalled, however, that there are marked differences in the perceived importance of the sales effort facet of competitive strategy. Manufacturers of fabricated parts and materials placed the most emphasis, and aerospace and defense contractors the least emphasis, on the sales effort facet.

Distribution Activities

Because of the relatively small number of buyers and sellers and the large amount of money involved in the typical industrial goods transaction, these products are usually sold through relatively short channels of distribution. In many instances, the manufacturer deals directly with the customer and no intermediaries are involved. Another factor encouraging the use of a short channel is the great importance of the transaction and the product to the buyer. If the product, such as a packaging machine, fails to function properly, the purchaser's production line may have to be shut down. Similarly, a relatively small fabricated part may be essential to the purchaser's operations. If it does not conform to specifications, the product of which it is a part may fail to function properly. As a result, warranty and postsale service costs will rise, while customers' goodwill is likely to fall. For these and other reasons, industrial goods purchasers usually prefer to deal directly with their suppliers, and, in many

[76]

instances, the executives of the purchasing company are involved in the buying decision and transaction.

Although the utilization of short channels of distribution decreases the importance of activities pertaining to middlemen, it tends to increase the importance of the physical supply functions. Industrial goods producers dealing directly with their customers must assume most of the responsibility for storage and transportation.[2] Therefore, it is not surprising to find that the industrial goods respondents allocated most of their distribution points to the physical supply functions.

As shown in Table VI-5, the industrial goods producers allocated from 45 to 71 of their distribution points to warehousing, inventory control and transportation. Aerospace and defense contractors and industrial chemical producers allocated 37 and 44 points, respectively, to transportation. Manufacturers of capital goods and fabricated parts and materials allocated 17 and 21 of their distribution points, respectively, to transportation. It should be recalled, however, that the overall distribution facet represents only one percent of the total competitive strategy of the aerospace and defense contractors, while representing 11 percent of the total strategy of the other three types of producers.

Warehousing and inventory control received only 14 points from aerospace and defense contractors, but they received from 28 to 31 points from the other three types of industrial goods producers. This element of distribution was most important to fabricators of parts and materials.

Determination, selection, and development of the channels of distribution received 51 points from manufacturers of capital goods, 42 from fabricators of parts and materials, 36 points from aerospace and defense contractors, and 27 points from producers of industrial chemicals. Among these three distributor-related activities, assistance to and development of channels of distribution was most important, especially to producers of capital goods.

---

[2] In some instances, however, the purchaser will assume part of the storage function. This is particularly true in the case of fabricated parts and materials and industrial chemicals.

Selection of establishments within the channels of distribution was also more important to capital goods producers than to producers in the other three industrial goods industries.

Table VI–5

RELATIVE IMPORTANCE OF THE ELEMENTS OF DISTRIBUTION

Distribution Activity	Aerospace and Defense	Capital Goods	Industrial Chemicals	Fabricated Parts and Materials
Warehousing and Inventory Control	14.0	28.1	27.6	30.9
Transportation	37.2	16.9	43.6	21.0
Determination of Channels	6.0	10.4	10.8	11.2
Selection of Establishments in the Channels	13.0	15.0	7.5	13.7
Assistance to and Development of the Channels	16.5	25.8	8.6	17.2
Other Distribution Activities	13.3	3.8	1.9	6.0
Total Distribution	100.0	100.0	100.0	100.0

Pricing Policies

The primary motive in the purchase of industrial goods is profit. Buyers of industrial goods use the capital equipment, fabricated parts, and the other items they purchase for the operation of their businesses. As Joel Dean has observed, profits are the acid test of a business. While this statement definitely does not imply that profit is the only motive in the purchase of industrial goods, or the only motive of the businessman, it does realistically suggest that potential profits are a primary incentive for the purchase of industrial goods.

Although the prices paid are a major determinant of the production costs of an industrial goods purchaser, it does not follow that price is his major consideration. First and foremost, industrial goods buyers are concerned with the reliability of their suppliers and the products they purchase from them.[3] Product quality, product service, reliable deliveries, accurate information about the product, and other nonprice factors usually are far

[3] J. H. Westing, I. V. Fine, and Gary Joseph Zenz, *Purchasing Management,* Third Edition, (New York: John Wiley & Sons, Inc., 1969), pp. 79-102.

more important than the small savings to be derived from a lower price. On the other hand, if a number of suppliers can satisfy the purchaser's nonprice requirements, his order is likely to go to the lowest bidder. In short, price is important to the industrial goods buyer, but it is far from being his most important consideration. Consequently, the typical industrial goods manufacturer attributed only about 20 percent of his product's success to the pricing facet of marketing strategy.

The pricing facet may be subdivided into a number of specific strategies or policies. Most companies, particularly the smaller firms in the industry, are not likely to be price leaders. If their products are fairly similar to those of competitors, they are likely to adopt the prevailing price in the industry. Any change in price is likely to be initiated by one of the stronger firms in the industry. Still, when products are similar, even the industry leaders may have to conform to the prices of others. The most a price leader can do is to attempt to initiate a price change. If the rest of the industry adopts an increased price suggested by the leader, a new level of prices will be established. If not, the leader will have to rescind the price increase. As for decreases, almost any member of the industry can lead prices down during periods of excess capacity.

In light of the above, one would expect that most companies would tend to price according to competitive levels, and as shown in Table VI-6, this expectation is realized in all but the aerospace and defense industry. Producers of industrial chemicals allocated, on the average, 59 points to this pricing policy; fabricated parts and capital goods manufacturers allocated 56 and 39 points, respectively, to pricing according to competitive levels. However, this approach to pricing was relatively unimportant to defense and aerospace contractors, as they allocated only 15 points to it. Instead, they emphasized government rules and regulations in establishing their prices.

In general, the second most important pricing policy in the success of industrial goods was cost-plus, or standard cost pricing. Capital goods producers relied heavily on this approach and allocated one-third of their points to it. Industrial chemical producers placed the least emphasis on cost-plus pricing, allocating

[79]

Table VI–6

RELATIVE IMPORTANCE OF VARIOUS PRICING POLICIES

Pricing Policies	Aerospace and Defense	Capital Goods	Industrial Chemicals	Fabricated Parts and Materials
Pricing According to Competitive Levels	14.6	39.4	58.6	56.1
Cost-Plus Pricing	20.7	33.3	16.3	21.3
Pricing According to What Market Will Bear	10.6	13.9	16.5	12.5
Pricing Above or Below Competitive Prices	4.7	8.6	7.1	5.4
Prices Based on Government Rules & Regulations	49.5	4.4	1.4	4.6
Other Pricing Policies	.0	.4	.0	.0
Total Pricing Strategy	100.0	100.0	100.0	100.0

only 16 points to that pricing strategy.

Next in general importance was pricing according to what the market will bear. However, producers of industrial chemicals placed slightly more emphasis on this approach than on cost-plus pricing, making it second in importance among these firms.

One would expect that the products of some firms would have a marketing advantage over the products of their rivals. The firms enjoying a competitive advantage probably would have some degree of pricing freedom and might follow the policy of pricing a certain percent or amount above the prevailing level of prices in the industry. Conversely, firms suffering from a disadvantage might be forced to adopt the policy of charging somewhat less than the general price level of the industry. The point allocations to the policy of pricing above or below the general prevailing level indicate that the strategy was used, but not to any great extent. Capital goods producers placed the most emphasis on this policy, but allocated only nine points to it. It should be recognized, however, that a firm with a favorable product differentiation might express this advantage by charging what the market will bear, or by charging the competitive price and reaping a higher than average volume of sales and share of market.

The freedom to differentiate one's price from those of competitors is probably best represented by the total points allocated

to cost-plus pricing, pricing according to what the market will bear, and pricing above and below competitors' prices. The measure obtained is far from perfect because management might elect to price according to competitive levels even though it had some freedom to vary prices. With this limitation in mind, it is noteworthy that capital goods producers apparently have the greatest pricing freedom. They allocated 56 points to the three pricing policies, while producers of industrial chemicals and fabricated parts allocated 40 and 39 points, respectively, to policies other than pricing according to competitive levels and government regulations.

One may speculate about the effect that a reliance upon government rules and regulations has on the prices of aerospace and defense products. The government is a monopsony, and the number of qualified suppliers is few; therefore, any resemblance to a competitive market may be impossible. However, with the relatively small emphasis placed on the prices of competitors, one wonders if the prices of aerospace and defense equipment are generally above or below those which would prevail in a more usual market situation. Also, what is the direction and magnitude of the deviation? Unfortunately, this research cannot provide an answer to these questions, which are important to both industry and the public.[4]

We now turn to the importance of the specific marketing activities in the total competitive strategy of the industrial goods manufacturers.

Relative Importance of Specific Marketing Activities

Although information was obtained on 20 components of product effort, sales effort, distribution, and pricing, closely related activities have been combined, yielding ten major marketing activities. The importance of these activities was calculated by multiplying the number of points received by each of them times the number of points received by the major facet to which the activity belongs. The relative importance of various marketing activities in the four industries is shown in Table VI-7.

---

[4] For an expanded discussion of this and other topics concerning pricing, see Chapter VIII.

Table VI–7

PERCEIVED IMPORTANCE OF SPECIFIC MARKETING ACTIVITIES IN THE TOTAL STRATEGY OF INDUSTRIAL GOODS PRODUCERS

Marketing Activity	Aerospace and Defense	Capital Goods	Industrial Chemicals	Fabricated Parts and Materials
Sales Management & Personal Selling	19.6	25.3	32.9	31.5
Advertising	3.0	6.0	4.5	5.8
Other Marketing Communications	3.7	7.4	4.9	8.2
Determination, Selection & Development of Distribution Channels	.5	5.7	3.3	5.4
Physical Distribution	.8	4.8	7.8	5.9
Product Service	16.3	13.4	9.7	10.7
Technical R & D	24.6	10.2	9.1	8.2
Other Product Efforts	9.0	7.3	8.1	6.1
Pricing According to Competitive Levels	3.2	7.5	11.5	10.3
Other Pricing Strategies	18.4	11.6	8.1	8.0
Other Marketing Activities	1.0	.8	.0	.0
Total Competitive Strategy	100.0	100.0	100.0	100.0

Sales management and personal selling is the most important marketing activity in the success of industrial goods sold to private industry; and it is second most important in the marketing of aerospace and defense equipment purchased by the government. (Even the latter producers attributed 20 percent of their strategy to sales management.) Manufacturers of industrial chemicals allocated 25 percent of their total competitive strategy points to sales management, while producers of fabricated parts and chemicals allocated 32 and 33 points, respectively, to this component of marketing strategy.

First in perceived importance to aerospace and defense contractors is technical R & D, which received 25 percent of their total strategy points. This is not surprising in light of the highly technical products which they are called upon to design and produce for national aerospace and defense programs. In general, their products are far more technical than those of the other three industries. Pricing policies, other than pricing at the competitive level, (primarily pricing according to government regu-

lations) are third in importance in the marketing success of the defense and aerospace products, and product service is rated fourth. Although all the activities shown in Table VI-7 are essential in the marketing programs of most firms, no activity, other than those mentioned, is of relatively great importance to producers of aerospace and defense equipment.

The point allocations of capital goods producers indicate that product service is second in importance, receiving 13 percent of the total strategy points, and that pricing strategies other than pricing at the competitive level are third. If all pricing strategies were considered as one marketing activity, then pricing would be second in importance. Technical R & D is perceived as fourth in importance among these producers.

Pricing according to competitive levels is second in perceived importance among the industrial chemical producers, product service is third, and technical R & D fourth.

Manufacturers of fabricated parts and materials indicated that product service is second most important in their marketing success; however, if all pricing strategies were combined, they would place second. Without combining, pricing according to competitive levels is third in perceived importance among the ten major marketing activities. Technical R & D and marketing communications other than sales management and advertising are tied for fourth in importance in the marketing of fabricated parts and materials.

In summary, sales management, product service, pricing, and technical R & D are perceived to be the four most important activities in the competitive strategies and marketing success of all four types of industrial goods producers.

Conclusion

The majority of the questionnaires and data which provide the empirical basis of this study came from four industrial goods industries. Fortunately, the product-market of each of these industries is fairly homogeneous. Although all four industries had relatively sophisticated product-markets (average profiles ranging from 1.2 to 1.9), the differences among their product-market profiles were predictive of the differences in their marketing

[83]

strategies. The importance of the product facet of competitive strategy did vary directly with the sophistication of the product-market, being most important among aerospace and defense contractors and next most important among manufacturers of capital goods. The importance of the sales effort facet varied inversely with the sophistication of the product-market, being most important among fabricators of parts and materials and second most important among industrial chemical producers. Therefore, the product-market model is vigorously supported by the point allocations of the industrial goods producers.

A noteworthy empirical finding is the relatively high emphasis that the industrial goods industries placed on a specific marketing activity—sales management and personal selling. With the exception of aerospace and defense producers, this activity was perceived as being of substantially greater importance than any other marketing activity.

CHAPTER VII

MARKETING STRATEGIES FOR
CONSUMER GOODS

In this chapter we shall examine the marketing strategies for five types of consumer goods: consumer chemicals (primarily drugs); consumer durables (primarily appliances); petroleum products; food, liquor and tobacco products; and other nondurables such as textiles, paper, and household supplies. As will be shown, the competitive strategies of consumer goods manufacturers differ significantly from each other and from those who market industrial goods.

Nature Of Consumer Markets

The market for consumer goods is composed of many buyers who are not specialists in purchasing. Furthermore, consumers purchase a vast array of widely differing products; therefore their knowledge of any one product tends to be low relative to that of the industrial purchaser. The values of the products bought are frequently too low to justify extensive purchasing effort. The buying motives are often predominantly socio-psychological in nature, and many consumer products are not particularly complex. Consequently, the product-markets are considerably less sophisticated than those for industrial goods. As shown in Table VII-1, the executives participating in the study considered the product-market for consumer chemicals to be the most sophisticated of the five types of consumer goods studied. This could be due to the number of prescription drugs producers among the consumer chemical respondents and the fact that physicians' pre-

scriptions are a major factor in the demand for these products. However, the major factors contributing to the relatively high sophistication of this product-market were the purchase motives of consumers and the products' complexity. Buying motives were judged to be more operational than socio-psychological (1.6); and the average product was, by a considerable margin, more complex than the other types of consumer products included in the sample.

Table VII-1

PRODUCT-MARKET PROFILES FOR SELECTED CONSUMER GOODS*

Type of Product	Average Profile	Buyer Knowledge	Buyer Effort	Purchase Motives	Product Complexity
Consumer Chemicals	2.2	2.2	3.3	1.6	1.7
Consumer Durables	2.6	2.6	2.7	2.3	2.8
Petroleum Products	2.8	3.2	4.2	1.6	2.3
Food, Liquor & Tobacco	3.3	2.0	4.2	1.6	4.0
Other Nondurables	3.0	2.2	4.0	2.3	3.6

	1	2	3	4	5
Key:					

Very Sophisticated (e.g., Great Buyer Effort)	Moderately Sophisticated (e.g., Moderate Buyer Effort)	Very Non-sophisticated (e.g., Minimal Buyer Effort)

*The profiles are based on responses from 13 consumer chemical manufacturers, 44 producers of durables, 18 petroleum product manufacturers, 30 producers of food, liquor and tobacco products, and 18 manufacturers of other consumer nondurables.

The next most sophisticated product-market, as determined by the respondents' ratings, was that of consumer durable goods. Consumers' knowledge and purchasing efforts, and the product complexity of the durable goods, were judged to be slightly more than moderately sophisticated. The buying motives for consumer durables were considered to be more operational than socio-psychological; however, both types of buying motives were seen as significant in the purchase decisions of consumers.

The product-market profile for petroleum products was third most sophisticated. Consumer buying knowledge was slightly less than moderate, while buying efforts were considered to be minimal (4.2). The latter is due to the fact that gasoline and other

consumer petroleum products are usually bought on a convenience basis with little searching and shopping effort involved. Product complexity was judged to be more than moderate, and purchasers motives were primarily functional, rather than socio-psychological in nature.

Food, liquor and tobacco products had, on the average, the least sophisticated product-market of all the products included in the research. The slightly less than moderate sophistication of the average profile (3.3) was due to the relatively low degree of product complexity and, even more so, to the convenience nature of the products. As indicated by the food, liquor, and tobacco industry executives, consumers extend very little effort in making the purchase of these products. As for the consumers' buying motives, operational and socio-psychological motives were considered to be about equally important. Buyer knowledge concerning food, liquor, and tobacco products was the most extensive of the five types of consumer goods. This knowledge is probably a function of the frequency of purchase and the ability of consumers to judge whether the products yield the desired taste and other satisfactions which they are seeking.

Other consumer nondurable goods had a product-market profile which was somewhat similar to that of the food and related products industry. Because most of the goods involved were of a convenience nature, such as paper products, buyer effort was low. The products were relatively non-technical, and buyers' knowledge was somewhat more than moderate. Purchaser motives were perceived as being more operational than socio-psychological in nature.

Limitations of the Sample

The samples for the consumer goods industries are not as good as those for the industrial goods industries discussed in the preceding chapter. First, the consumer goods samples are, in most instances, smaller than those for the industrial products. Secondly, the responses for like products were not as consistent as those of the industrial producers. This is undoubtedly due, at least in part, to the fact that the product groupings are not highly homogeneous. For example, the product-markets and competitive strategies for basic food products are not highly similar to those of

champagne and other liquor products. However, somewhat unlike products had to be combined in order to obtain an adequate sample size. The small samples for each product type are due to the larger assortment of consumer goods industries, and the fact that the response ratio from consumer goods manufacturers was substantially less than that of the industrial goods producers.

A somewhat disturbing factor in the product-market evaluations by the consumer goods manufacturers (Table VII-1) was the lack of homogeneity in the response of some manufacturers having highly similar goods. For example, one tire manufacturer rated automobile tires as highly complex (a scale value of one), whereas another rated it as relatively nontechnical (a scale value of four). There appeared to be a tendency among *some* of the consumer goods respondents to rate their product-markets as more sophisticated than they actually were.

For the above reasons, little attempt will be made to test the product-market model with the consumer goods data. The responses from these producers have already been used in the tests presented in Chapter V. To make further use of somewhat dubious product-market evaluations is not warranted.

Even though the product-market evaluations sometimes lacked consistency, this does not impair the value of the marketing strategy allocations. Because the author knows of no better information on the relative importance of the various elements of the marketing mix of consumer goods manufacturers, the data will be presented and discussed.

The Competitive Strategies

As shown in Table VII-2, producers of drugs and other consumer chemicals attributed more importance to the product facet of competition than did the other producers of consumer goods. The consumer chemical industry emphasis on product effort is to be anticipated, given its relatively sophisticated product-market.[1] However, the most important contributors to the suc-

---

[1] However, the product effort allocations of some other consumer goods industries did not vary directly with the relative sophistication of their product-markets.

cess of drugs and other consumer chemical products were sales management, advertising, and other sales effort activities. The executives allocated an average of 45 points to the sales effort facet of competitive strategy. Pricing, which was third in importance, and distribution were considered less important in the marketing of consumer chemicals than in the marketing of the other types of consumer goods.

Table VII–2

PERCEIVED IMPORTANCE OF THE MAJOR FACETS OF COMPETITIVE STRATEGY AMONG CONSUMER GOODS PRODUCERS

Major Facet	Consumer Chemicals	Consumer Durables	Petroleum Products	Food, Liquor, & Tobacco	Other Nondurables
Product Effort	29.4	24.6	15.3	25.8	22.8
Sales Effort	45.1	36.4	46.1	44.6	45.0
Distribution	11.9	19.4	18.1	14.6	17.8
Pricing	13.6	19.3	20.6	14.9	14.4
Other	.0	.2	.0	.0	.0
Total Competitive Strategy	100.0	100.0	100.0	100.0	100.0

Producers of consumer durable goods placed less emphasis on sales effort than did the other types of consumer goods producers. However, sales effort was perceived to be more important than the other three major facets of marketing strategy. While sales effort received 36 points, the executives attributed about one-fourth of their marketing success to the product facet of competition. The remaining points were split equally between distribution and pricing. The distribution facet was judged more important in the marketing of consumer durables than in the marketing of the other types of consumer goods.

Product effort was considered to be the least important facet in the success of petroleum products. Petroleum product executives allocated an average of only 15 points to product effort. On the other hand, sales effort and pricing were more important in the marketing of petroleum products than for the other types of consumer goods. Sales effort received an average of 46 points and pricing received almost 21 points among the petroleum product producers.

Sales effort, with 45 points, was most important in the success of food, liquor, and tobacco products, and product effort (with almost 26 points) was also relatively important. Both distribution and pricing received slightly less than 15 points.

Producers of other consumer nondurable goods placed the most emphasis on sales effort and the least on pricing.

In summary, all types of consumer goods producers emphasized sales effort in the success of their products. With the exception of petroleum products, product effort was second in importance among the industries. In general, distribution and pricing were perceived to be about equally important and less important than the other two facets.

Product Strategies

Manufacturers of consumer chemicals emphasized the technical research and development of new and existing products more than any other product effort activity. However, it is interesting to find that these respondents considered market research as also highly important in the success of their products. As shown in Table VII-3, technical research and development received an average of 38 points and market research received 29.

Information on expenditure patterns of industry indicates that United States corporations are relying increasingly on market research for the evaluation of new products and product proposals. An economist studying annual research and development expenditures for Battelle Memorial Institute points out that businessmen are using market studies "to offset their research departments' feverish and often impractical pursuit of ideas for ideas' sake."[2] The scientists in our nation's R & D laboratories should be expected to pursue ideas for the sake of knowledge. From these pursuits have come some of the most important and profitable products of American industry. However, market research is needed to evaluate and guide the development of the products which are conceived by exploratory research.

Far too many products are developed which do not provide

---

[2] "Firms Strive to Avoid Introducing Products that Nobody Will Buy," *Wall Street Journal,* March 6, 1967, p. 1.

adequate satisfaction for their intended markets. For example, the American Gas Association spent $200,000 developing a conveyerized gas toaster that toasted 16 slices of bread at a time, a coffee maker that could brew from one cup to several gallons of coffee, and some unique food warmers *before* a marketing study showed that restaurants wouldn't purchase the appliances.[3] If it hadn't been for market research, the loss would have been far greater than $200,000. However, had market research been used to investigate the market potential of these ideas while they were still in the embryo state, the loss could have been reduced substantially.

Marketing research and technical research should work as a team throughout the development of most new products. In this way, the developing product is continually evaluated and is more likely to emerge from the R & D process with characteristics which will be desired by consumers. As a result, the likely returns from research and development are greatly enhanced. Risk of product failure is reduced and the probability of success is increased. Also, market research is frequently useful in the design of the promotional strategy which is used to launch the new or improved product. In other words, market research is a key to the development, growth, and profitability of a product. Therefore, it is not surprising to find that market research was second only to technical R & D in the product activities of all five types of consumer goods manufacturers.[4] Also, it is not surprising to find a greater reliance on market reseach among consumer goods producers than industrial goods manufacturers. Consumer producers usually have less rapport with their customers because of their large numbers and long channels of distribution. However, there are many industrial goods producers that could benefit from a greater reliance on market research.

---

[3] *Ibid.*

[4] However, if pre- and postsale service are combined, their perceived importance outranks market research in the consumer durable and petroleum products industries.

Table VII-3

RELATIVE IMPORTANCE OF THE ELEMENTS
OF PRODUCT STRATEGY IN CONSUMER GOODS INDUSTRIES

Product Effort Activity	Consumer Chemicals	Consumer Durables	Petroleum Products	Food, Liquor, & Tobacco	Other Nondurables
Technical R & D	38.1	35.5	40.3	39.8	33.2
Presale Service	14.2	12.2	14.4	8.6	12.3
Postsale Service	7.7	12.7	16.7	4.5	8.2
Market Research	29.2	18.8	19.6	31.0	32.4
Style R & D	10.8	18.7	1.1	14.3	12.8
Other Product Efforts	.0	2.0	7.9	1.7	1.1
Total Product Strategy	100.0	100.0	100.0	100.0	100.0

Producers of consumer durable goods (primarily appliances) emphasized technical R & D in their product effort and placed less emphasis on market research than the other types of consumer goods manufacturers. However, their total emphasis on research was substantial because of the importance attributed to a third category of research, style R & D. All product research activities received 73 percent of the product strategy points of the durable goods producers. The majority of the remaining points went to pre- and postsale service.

Manufacturers of petroleum products placed greater emphasis on technical R & D and product service than the other types of consumer goods producers. This was due, in part, to the lack of importance of style R & D in the marketing of petroleum products. It should be recalled that this group of producers placed the least emphasis on the overall product facet of competitive strategy.

Processors of food, liquor, and tobacco products allocated 71 percent of their product effort points to technical R & D and market research. Style R & D and product service shared the remaining points and were considered about equally important.

Technical R & D and market research were visualized as about equally important by the producers of other nondurable goods —each receiving about one-third of the product effort points. Style R & D received 13 of the remaining points.

In summary, technical R & D and market research pertaining to product development are, respectively, first and second in importance to all five types of consumer goods producers. How-

ever, if pre- and postsale service are combined, they are visualized as second in importance to manufacturers of consumer durables and petroleum products. Given the relative importance attributed to market research in the product strategy of the companies studied, the returns from market research expenditures must be quite high. It is estimated that industry spent less than $500 million on market studies in 1966.[5] This is far less than expenditures on technical R & D and product service.

Marketing Communication Programs

Of the points to be allocated among the various elements of sales effort strategy, over one-half were assigned to sales management and personal selling by producers of consumer chemicals (Table VII-4). One-third were assigned to advertising, with printed media being considered more important than broadcast media advertising. The majority of the remaining 16 points were allocated to branding and promotional packaging.

Table VII-4

MARKETING COMMUNICATIONS AMONG CONSUMER GOODS PRODUCERS

Sales Effort Activity	Consumer Chemicals	Consumer Durables	Petroleum Products	Food, Liquor, & Tobacco	Other Nondurables
Sales Management and Personal Selling	51.9	45.8	47.8	24.1	37.1
Printed Media Advertising	19.0	16.3	10.0	14.2	14.6
Broadcast Media Advertising	13.5	11.8	16.4	30.2	22.1
Special Promotional Activities	6.9	15.6	16.1	18.9	14.4
Branding and Promotional Packaging	7.9	10.3	8.1	11.6	11.1
Other Sales Efforts	.8	.2	1.7	1.0	.7
Total Sales Efforts	100.0	100.0	100.0	100.0	100.0

Consumer durable goods manufacturers attributed somewhat less importance to sales management and advertising. However, sales management received about 46 percent of the sales effort

[5] *Ibid.*

points, and advertising received 28 percent. Again, printed media were judged as more important in marketing success than the broadcast media. Special promotional activities were quite important to this group of producers, receiving 16 points.

Producers of petroleum products also emphasized sales management and personal selling in their marketing communications programs. Advertising received 26 points, with the broadcast media being visualized as more important than printed media advertising. However, special promotional activities received about as many points as broadcast media advertising and more points than printed media advertising.

The food, liquor, and tobacco industry placed less emphasis on sales management and personal selling than the other types of producers. Less than one-fourth of their sales success was attributed to sales management. Broadcast media advertising was considered especially important in the marketing communications for food and related products. While broadcast media advertising received over 30 percent of the sales effort points, all advertising received over 44 points. Both special promotional activities and branding and promotional packaging were judged more important in the food industry than in the other consumer goods industries.

Producers of other consumer nondurables placed substantial emphasis on both sales management and advertising. However, the prior was most important to this group.

In summary, sales management and personal selling were considered most important in the marketing communications for four of the five types of consumer goods industries. While advertising was most important in the food, liquor and tobacco industries, it was second most important in the other four industries. With the exception of consumer chemicals, special promotional activities were perceived as more important than branding and promotional packaging.

Distribution Activities

Manufacturers of drugs and other consumer chemicals considered the physical supply functions quite important in their distribution activities.

Table VII–5

RELATIVE IMPORTANCE OF THE ELEMENTS OF DISTRIBUTION AMONG CONSUMER GOODS PRODUCERS

Distribution Activity	Consumer Chemicals	Consumer Durables	Petroleum Products	Food, Liquor, & Tobacco	Other Nondurables
Warehousing and Inventory Control	32.7	21.5	10.7	30.5	24.4
Transportation	13.8	12.1	37.9	32.5	14.1
Determination of Channels	17.7	15.4	11.7	9.7	16.2
Selection of Establishment in the Channels	11.9	21.4	21.4	9.3	14.4
Assistance to and Development of the Channels	23.8	27.7	18.3	18.0	30.9
Other Distribution Activities	.0	1.8	.0	.0	.0
Total Distribution	100.0	100.0	100.0	100.0	100.0

As shown in Table VII-5, the majority of the 47 points going to physical supply were allocated to warehousing and inventory control rather than transportation. Because the products are small and light, transportation undoubtedly is not a major cost item in the consumer chemical industry. However, inventory control may be a major problem because of the many products and distributors involved, as well as possible deterioration of the product. The determination, selection, and development of channels of distribution received 53 points, with assistance to and development of channels being more important than the other two types of distributor related activities.

Durable goods producers attributed relatively little importance to the physical supply functions. About two-thirds of the 34 points allocated to physical supply went to warehousing and inventory control. These producers assigned 65 points to the determination, selection, and development of channels of distribution. Twenty-eight of these points went to assisting and developing the channels of distribution.

Producers of petroleum products split their distribution points about equally between physical supply and channel of distribution activities. Because of the bulky nature of their products, particularly gasoline and fuel oil, transportation is significantly

more important than the other four types of distribution activities. Selection of individual establishments within their channels of distribution was considered the second most important distribution activity of the petroleum industry producers.

The physical supply activities were of greatest importance to processors of food, liquor, and tobacco. Of the 63 points allocated to physical supply, slightly more than half went to transportation. Almost one-half of the 37 points going to channel of distribution activities went to assisting and developing the channel of distribution.

The relative lack of importance attributed to channel of distribution activities by the food industry may be due to the fact that many food, liquor, and tobacco items are pulled through the channel by consumer advertising and special promotions. The demands of the ultimate consumer are an important determinant of which national brands a retailer will carry. As for privately branded items, working with the channel would not be especially important in the marketing success of the manufacturer. In this case, the manufacturer concentrates on selling his product to the corporate retail chain or wholesaler who is doing the private branding. Once the sale is made, the private brander handles the dissemination of the product to the channel of distribution.

Neither the determination of channels or the selection of individual establishments should be very important to the food, liquor, and tobacco industries. These are, in general, convenience goods purchased with a minimum of effort by consumers. Because of this, the producers should concentrate on developing an intensive distribution system for their products. Therefore, they should distribute through as many channels and as many retail establishments within each channel as possible. In the author's opinion, most consumer convenience goods producers should get their products into as many retail outlets and on as many different shelves of each outlet as possible to achieve maximum sales success. In addition, the manufacturer should strive to obtain maximum retail shelf space and to obtain a favorable location in the retail establishment. These suggestions are especially important for those products for which consumers do not have strong preferences or brand loyalties. When brand

[96]

preferences are weak, the manufacturer with the most retail outlets and the most favorable shelf space (in terms of quality and quantity) is likely to have the largest share of the market.

Because of the above, the determination of which channels to use and the selection of individual establishments within the channels should not be particularly important to food and other convenience goods manufacturers. However, assisting and developing channels of distribution should be quite important. The point allocations suggest that this is the case.

Manufacturers of other nondurable goods allocated 38 percent of their distribution points to physical supply activities, and 62 percent to channel of distribution activities. Of most importance to this group is assisting and developing the channels of distribution. Warehousing and inventory control were considered second in importance.

Pricing Policies

The pricing strategies of consumer goods manufacturers vary considerably from industry to industry. Differences in the market structures of the industries may be important, as suggested by traditional economic theory. Those industries consisting of many small competitors may follow different pricing strategies than those composed of a few large firms or a small number of large and small firms (oligopolistic situations).

Probably more important than the number of competitors, are variations in the degree of product differentiation within each industry. When the products of rival firms are recognized as being similar, there is little opportunity for any policy other than pricing according to competitive levels or collusion. The latter approach is, of course, clearly illegal. In those instances where the products of rival firms are differentiated, there is an opportunity to adopt pricing strategies other than pricing according to competitive levels. With this thought, or hypothesis, we turn to Table VII-6 which shows the pricing policies of the various types of consumer goods producers.

Pricing according to competitive levels is considered to be the most important pricing policy used by four of the five categories of producers. However, the relative importance of this

policy in the total pricing strategy varies substantially from industry to industry. Manufacturers of miscellaneous nondurable goods allocated only 33 points, while producers of petroleum products allocated 76 points to pricing according to competitive levels. This was the only pricing policy of major importance in

Table VII–6

RELATIVE IMPORTANCE OF THE ELEMENTS OF PRICING STRATEGY AMONG CONSUMER GOODS PRODUCERS

Pricing Policies	Consumer Chemicals	Consumer Durables	Petroleum Products	Food, Liquor, & Tobacco	Other Nondurables
Pricing According to Competitive Levels	43.3	44.3	75.5	39.0	32.5
Cost-Plus Pricing	20.0	27.7	10.3	29.2	40.0
Pricing According to What Market Will Bear	20.4	16.5	4.4	15.3	16.1
Pricing Above or Below Competitor's Prices	15.0	8.3	4.4	16.3	10.0
Prices Based on Government Rules and Regulations	1.3	3.1	5.3	.2	1.4
Total Pricing Strategy	100.0	100.0	100.0	100.0	100.0

the petroleum industry. Given the substantial similarity of petroleum products, one would, as suggested earlier, expect very little freedom to utilize any policy other than following the competitive price. Most consumers are probably aware of the fact that the bulk petroleum products of several different producers are often transported in a common pipe and that differences between their products, due to refining or the addition of additives, probably are not great. Because the resulting interdependence among the major competitors is so great, there is little opportunity to deviate from the prevailing level of prices.

Producers of drug products and other consumer chemicals enjoy a higher degree of product differentiation, although some of the differentiation may be due to fancied rather than real product differences. In addition, a few drug products have a quasi-monopoly position due to patent protection. In any event, con-

sumer chemical producers allocated 43 points to pricing according to competitive levels and 20 points to both cost-plus pricing and pricing according to what the market will bear. Another 15 percent of the pricing strategy of these producers was attributed to pricing a certain percent (or amount) above or below the prices of most competitors.

Producers of consumer durables allocated 44 percent of their pricing strategy to pricing according to competitive levels; another 28 percent was attributed to cost-plus pricing. The only other policy of considerable importance was charging what the market will bear, which received about 17 points.

Food, liquor, and tobacco producers allocated 39 percent of their strategy to pricing according to competitive levels and another 29 percent to cost-plus pricing. Approximately 16 points were allocated to both charging what the market will bear and pricing above or below competitors' prices.

Producers of other consumer nondurables placed less emphasis on pricing according to competitive levels than the other types of producers. Their most important pricing policy was cost-plus pricing, which received 40 points. This was the only group of producers to emphasize cost-plus pricing more than any other pricing policy.

Summary

In Table VII-7, the specific marketing activities have been consolidated into 11 groups and weighted according to the point allocations of the major facet to which each activity belonged. The result is a picture of the perceived relative importance of each activity in the total competitive strategy of the firm.

Strategies for Consumer Chemicals

Sales management and personal selling is perceived as the most important specific marketing activity in the competitive strategy of the consumer chemical industry. Over 23 percent of the total importance of all marketing activities was attributed to selling. Advertising is considered second in importance. If all pricing policies are visualized as one marketing activity, pricing would be third in importance. Next in perceived importance is the

[99]

technical research and development of new and improved products. No other marketing activity received over 10 percent of the total points to be allocated among the various marketing activities. Receiving about 9 percent of the points was the use of market research in product development. In fact, the proprietory and prescription drug producers placed more emphasis on market research than any other industry.

Strategies for Consumer Durables

Sales management and personal selling is perceived as most important in the competitive strategies of appliance and other durable goods producers. However, if the points attributed to all pricing policies are combined, pricing would rank first in importance. The determination, selection and development of distribution channels are next in perceived importance. The only other category to receive over 10 percent of the points allocated by consumer durable goods manufacturers was printed and broadcast media advertising.

Strategies for Petroleum Products

Executives of the petroleum industry visualize sales management and personal selling as most important in the success of their products. Second in importance is pricing according to competitive levels, which received almost 16 percent of their points. Advertising ranks third in significance for the petroleum industry. No other specific activity received over 10 percent of the points; however, the combination of special promotions and branding received 12 points. The determination, selection, and development of distribution channels and physical distribution were also considered relatively important by this industry.

Strategies for Food, Liquor, and Tobacco

In the food, liquor and tobacco industry, advertising is visualized as being the most important activity in the success of a product. Almost 20 percent of the importance of all marketing activities was attributed to broadcast and printed media adver-

Table VII–7

PERCEIVED IMPORTANCE OF SPECIFIC MARKETING ACTIVITIES IN THE TOTAL STRATEGY OF CONSUMER GOODS PRODUCERS

Marketing Activity	Consumer Chemicals	Consumer Durables	Petroleum Products	Food, Liquor, & Tobacco	Other Nondurables
Sales Management and Personal Selling	23.4	16.7	22.0	10.7	16.7
Advertising	14.7	10.2	12.2	19.8	16.5
Other Sales Efforts	7.0	9.5	11.9	14.1	11.8
Determination, Selection and Development of Distribution Channels	6.4	12.5	9.3	5.4	10.9
Physical Distribution	5.5	6.5	8.8	9.2	6.9
Product Service	6.4	6.1	4.8	3.4	4.7
Technical R & D	11.2	8.7	6.2	10.3	7.6
Market Research	8.6	4.6	3.0	8.0	7.4
Other Product Efforts	3.2	5.2	1.4	4.1	3.1
Pricing According to Competitive Levels	5.9	8.6	15.6	5.8	4.7
Other Pricing Strategies	7.7	10.7	5.0	9.1	9.7
Other Marketing Activities	.0	.6	.0	.0	.0
Total Competitive Strategy	100.0	100.0	100.0	100.0	100.0

tising. If all pricing policies are considered as one activity, pricing would be second in importance. Almost equally important are other sales efforts which include special promotions, branding, and promotional packaging. Sales management and personal selling and technical R & D are considered to be fourth and fifth in importance. The other activities of fairly great significance to the food industry were physical distribution and market research.

Strategies for Other Consumer Nondurables

Producers of other consumer nondurables perceive sales management and personal selling and advertising to be about equally important and most significant in the success of their products. All pricing policies are next in importance. Special promotions, branding, packaging, and the selection and development of dis-

[101]

tribution channels are also relatively significant to this group of manufacturers.

Conclusion

The sales facet, and especially sales management and personal selling, is perceived as most significant in the marketing success of most of the consumer products included in this study. Distribution activities, pricing and advertising are also of relatively great significance. The importance of technical R & D varies considerably from industry to industry; it is most important in the drug and food industries.

CHAPTER VIII

PRICING STRATEGIES OF
UNITED STATES INDUSTRY

Despite the great emphasis placed on the nonprice facets of competitive strategy, pricing presents business management and our society with one of its most important and perplexing economic problems. A free enterprise or marketplace economy is predicated upon the assumption that the "invisible hand" of perfect competition will provide price protection for consumers and an optimum allocation of society's resources. However, the advancement of technology and resulting economies of large scale have made perfect competition, with its many producers, an inefficient form of industrial organization for most manufacturing industries. As a result, the typical U.S. manufacturer is in direct competition with only a few rival producers.

The Oligopoly Problem

In an oligopolistic situation where there is a small number of firms and products are similar, there is a high degree of interdependence and uncertainty. Interdependence prevails because the pricing decisions of any one company may have a profound effect on the sales and profits of the other firms in the industry. Unless there is an illegal collusive arrangement, uncertainty arises because of the unpredictability of the pricing behavior of rivals.[1] Suppose, for example, that a given industry has eight firms producing similar products and that five of these firms are currently operating at less than 80 percent of capacity. The financial executive of Firm A, operating at 73 percent of capacity, pro-

---

[1] For theoretical discussions of this situation, see Paul M. Sweezy, "Demand Under Conditions of Oligopoly," *The Journal of Political Economy*, XLVII (1939), pp. 568-573, and George J. Stigler, "The Kinky Oligopoly Demand Curve and Rigid Prices," *The Journal of Political Economy*, LV (1947), pp. 432-449.

Figure VIII–1

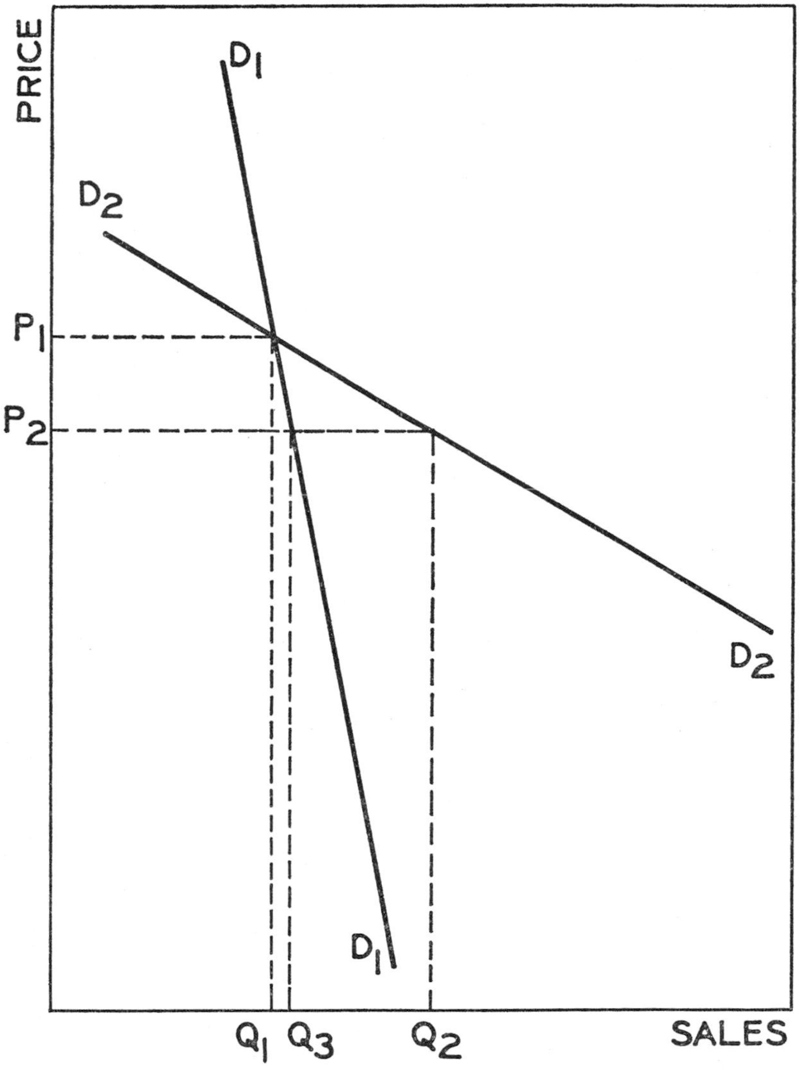

LEGEND FOR FIGURE VIII-1

D_1D_1 — Demand curve of Firm A, assuming all rivals charge the same price.

P_1 — Current price prevailing in the industry.

Q_1 — Current sales of Firm A at Price P_1.

D_2D_2 — Demand curve of Firm A, assuming all rivals continue to use Price P_1, even though Firm A changes its price.

P_2 — A proposed price which is less than the prevailing price in the industry.

Q_2 — Sales of Firm A that would result from Price P_2 if rivals continue to charge Price P_1.

Q_3 — Sales of Firm A that would result from Price P_2 if rivals were to also charge Price P_2.

poses a 2 percent reduction of price to increase the firm's sales. He believes that the firm has an elastic demand curve and additional sales will result from a reduced price. A lower price should bring forth additional buyers and, most important, it will draw customers away from rival firms. Therefore, the revenues (and profit) lost due to the 2 percent price reduction on each unit sold should be more than offset by the additional sales and revenue brought forth by the proposed change. Figure VIII-1 illustrates these assumptions.

The accuracy of the executive's estimates will depend upon the responsiveness of consumers to the reduction of price *and the reactions of the firm's rivals*. Should rivals maintain their current prices at P_1 even though Firm A reduces its price to P_2, the sales of Firm A should rise to Q_2. The difference between Q_2 and Q_3 represents the sales taken from rival companies. However, if rivals also reduce their prices to P_2, Firm A will experience only a small increase in sales $(Q_3 - Q_1)$, the size of the increase being dependent on the reaction of consumers to the general change in price (the elasticity of the industry's demand curve). On the other hand, rivals might react vigorously to Firm A's reduction of price. Should they retaliate by reducing prices below P_2, A's sales probably would decrease rather than increase, and an unprofitable and chaotic price war might commence. Therefore, the interdependence among the firms of an oligopolistic industry creates a very uncertain situation and a difficult pricing problem—one which generates an attitude of fear during periods of excess capacity.

Despite the extent of the problem, the increasing concentration of industry, and the importance of price levels to both business and consumers, relatively little is known about how management prices. While some information concerning the pricing strategies of the 485 responding companies has already been presented, the strategies and their utilization by U.S. industry will now be more carefully examined.

Strategies Available To The Firm

The business executive has numerous pricing strategies for establishing the price level of his company's products. One such policy, generally referred to as cost-plus pricing, involves pricing each unit of the product at cost of production and distribution plus some margin for profit. To use this method of price determination, one must assume a given volume of sales because overhead and other indirect costs per unit will vary inversely with the amount of production and sales. By assuming some standard volume of sales, the direct costs, indirect costs, and profit per unit may be calculated to derive a selling price. However, price is a major determinant of sales volume; so actual sales may vary substantially from the assumed standard volume. Consequently, profits may be far larger or smaller than targeted.

Despite its limitations, several industries (such as the automobile industry) claim they use the cost-plus approach in determining prices. An Oxford University study found this method to be the most widely used among British manufacturers.[2] However, in light of the interdependence among the rivals of an oligopolistic industry, it is difficult to visualize how anyone other than a price leader can place a heavy reliance on cost-plus pricing.

A second major strategy is pricing according to competitive levels. The competitive level is likely to be established by the interaction of supply and demand if there is a fairly large number of firms in the industry. If the number of firms is few, prices may be set by the larger or more respected firms in the industry which are regarded as price leaders. The other firms

---

[2] R. L. Hall and C. J. Hitch, "Price Theory and Business Behavior," *Oxford Studies in the Price Mechanism* (Oxford: Clarendon Press, Oxford University, 1951).

are price followers; their prices are established according to the price level of the leader or leaders in the industry.[3]

A somewhat related method of price determination is to price a certain percent above or below the price of most competitors. Relatively small firms can often price below the competitive level without retaliation so long as their share of market remains small. However, when such a firm threatens to take a considerable volume of sales away from its larger competitors, retaliation is likely.

A firm may also succeed in pricing below the competitive level if it has a product which is considered to be inferior to that of its competition. Conversely, a company with a product which is favorably differentiated may succeed in pricing its product higher than those of its rivals. In general, product differentiation, whether real or fancied, is the key to being able to price a certain percent above or below competitors.

Another strategy is to price according to what the market will bear. With this approach, management emphasizes profit maximization and the value of the product to potential customers. The price charged is supposedly the price which will yield the maximum profit for the company. This price can be fairly high if the demand for the product is highly inelastic (i.e., nonresponsive to various levels of price) and competition is lacking. On the other hand, the value approach can yield a fairly low price if demand is highly responsive to varying levels of price.

With the increasing involvement of government in the affairs of industry and, in some cases, the direct regulation of prices by public agencies, prices can be based on or influenced by government rules and regulations.

While other strategies or approaches may exist, these are the major policies or methods for determining prices. Typically,

---

[3] There are two basic types of price leaders—dominant firm and barometric. The prior is a leader because of its position and strength in the industry. For example, at one time United States Steel Corporation was considered to have so much power that it could dictate the prices of the steel industry. However, any such dominance is likely to be construed as monopolistic and illegal by the government anti-trust agencies. The barometric price leader does not have monopoly power, but frequently initiates price changes. Other firms usually follow this price leader because of their respect for the judgment of the firm, rather than fear of retaliation.

the pricing strategy used for a given product is likely to be a composit of two or more of the five major policies.

Pricing According To Competitive Level Most Important

As shown in Table VIII-1, pricing according to the competitive level was considered most important by the respondents. This strategy was perceived about equally important by all three major types of producers—industrial goods, consumer durable goods, and consumer nondurable goods—with an average of 46 points allocated to it.

In addition, some producers geared their prices to competitive levels, but were able to differentiate by pricing a certain percent above or below the generally prevailing market price. This strategy was most important to marketers of consumer nondurable goods, and least important to those marketing industrial goods. Therefore, it appears that product differentiation may be somewhat easier to obtain in consumer markets than in industrial markets.

If the points allocated to pricing according to the competitive level and pricing a certain percent above or below the competitive level are added, one finds that these approaches constitute, on the average, well over 50 percent of the pricing strategy of the firms studied. This is true of all three major types of producers.

Cost-Plus Pricing Second Most Important

Cost-plus pricing received over 25 percent of the points allocated by the corporate executives. Cost-plus, or standard cost, pricing was slightly more important to consumer goods manufacturers than it was to those producing industrial goods.

There was a fairly high degree of uniformity in the average perception of the importance of pricing according to what the market will bear. The three major types of manufacturers allocated approximately 14 points to this pricing strategy.

Pricing according to government rules and regulations was the least important element of pricing. As shown in Chapter VI, pricing according to government rules and regulations was highly important to a select group of industrial goods manufacturers.

Table VIII–1

THE PERCEIVED RELATIVE IMPORTANCE OF VARIOUS PRICING STRATEGIES

	Type of Product		
Pricing Strategy	Industrial	Consumer Durable	Consumer Nondurable
Competitive Level	46.7	45.0	46.0
Certain Percent Above or Below Competitive Level	6.7	8.1	11.1
Cost-Plus	25.1	28.2	27.1
What the Market Will Bear	13.4	15.8	14.2
According to Government Rules and Regulations	8.0	2.7	1.6
Other Strategies	.1	.1	—
Total Pricing Strategy	100.0	100.0	100.0

All other industrial and consumer goods producers placed very little emphasis on this aspect of pricing. However, the anti-trust element of government rules and regulations may have been a major factor in the emphasis placed on pricing according to competitive levels. In other words, the anti-trust laws and their enforcement may have helped to establish a competitive environment which forces most manufacturers to price competitively.

Structural Factors Have Little Impact

As shown in Chapter IV, the executives allocated, on the average, only 18 percent of their total strategy points to pricing. However, the perceived importance of pricing varied substantially from one company to another. As shown in Table VIII-2, 97 percent of allocations to pricing fell within the range of zero to 42.5 points.

In an attempt to explain the variation among the respondents' perceived importance of pricing, measurements of share of market, sales volume, and marketing costs were obtained. In each instance, the data pertained only to the product being studied, not the total company. Also, information was obtained on the size of the typical purchase (unit price times number of units in the average order). It was thought that these structural variables might have some impact on the relative importance of

[109]

Table VIII–2

PERCEIVED RELATIVE IMPORTANCE OF PRICING IN COMPETITIVE STRATEGY

Number of Points Allocated to Pricing	Percent of Total Respondents
Less than 2.5	8.3
2.5 to 7.5	9.6
7.5 to 12.5	20.0
12.5 to 17.5	8.1
17.5 to 22.5	22.1
22.5 to 27.5	13.3
27.5 to 32.5	9.8
32.5 to 37.5	1.7
37.5 to 42.5	4.2
42.5 and Over	2.9
Total Respondents	100.0

pricing in the total competitive strategy of the companies. Correlations were computed to make a quantitative evaluation of the possible relationship of the perceived importance of pricing to market share, sales volume, marketing costs, and size of typical purchase. The number of points allocated to pricing was the dependent variable.

Of the four independent variables, value of typical purchase was most closely related to the perceived importance of pricing. Although statistically significant,[4] the correlation coefficient was only .148. This means that only 2 percent of the total variation in the perceived importance of pricing can be explained by relating the number of points allocated to pricing to the value of typical purchase. Stated somewhat differently, there was a *slight* tendency for the importance of pricing to vary directly with the dollar volume of the typical purchase. However, 98 percent of the variation in the importance attributed to pricing remains unexplained. Furthermore, none of the remaining three variables could do as well in explaining the variation.

The correlation between share of market and perceived importance of pricing was —.043. The corresponding correlation coefficients for sales volume and marketing costs were —.035 and —.106, respectively. A multiple regression, using all four independent variables to explain the variation in the perceived importance of pricing, did not fare much better—the coefficient

[4] The T-value was 3.2973.

[110]

of multiple determination (percent of the variation in the importance of pricing explained by the four independent variables) was only 2.2 percent.

Importance Of Specific Pricing Strategies Varies By Industry

The relative importance attributed to the five approaches to price determination varied markedly among the various industries. (We are again viewing pricing strategy as equal to 100 points.) While some of the data shown in Table VIII-3 were presented in Chapters VI and VII, the table presents an overview of all the industries discussed earlier and adds some new industries.

The firms placing the most emphasis on pricing according to the competitive level were processors of raw materials. They allocated over 84 percent of their total pricing strategy points to competitive pricing. This is to be expected given the homogeneity of most raw materials and the ability of buyers to evaluate differences when they exist. To a lesser degree the same may be said for petroleum products, whose producers also emphasized competitive pricing. Manufacturers of chemicals and fabricated parts for the industrial market also placed relatively heavy emphasis on pricing according to competitive levels.

The aerospace and defense industries' executives allocated far fewer points to pricing at the competitive level than did the executives of other industries. This observation holds when the points allocated to pricing a certain percent above or below competitors are included in the comparison. While one might think that bidding for government contracts would make competitive pricing highly important, this evidently is *not* the case. The importance attributed to cost-plus pricing by the aerospace and defense contractors was also less than that of most other industries. Instead, the government-oriented industries placed primary emphasis on government rules and regulations.

Pricing a certain percent above or below the generally prevailing level of pricing was most heavily emphasized by producers of food, liquor, tobacco, and drug products. This is not unexpected, given the heavy emphasis of these industries on promotion and other means of differentiating their products in

[111]

Table VIII–3

RELATIVE IMPORTANCE OF FIVE PRICING STRATEGIES IN THIRTEEN MAJOR INDUSTRIES*

Type of Industry	Competitive Level	Above or Below the Competitive Level	Cost-Plus	What the Market Will Bear	According to Government Rules and Regulations
GOVERNMENT:					
Aerospace	13.9	6.4	18.9	13.6	47.1
Defense	15.1	3.1	22.3	7.7	51.7
INDUSTRIAL:					
Capital Goods	39.4	8.6	33.3	13.9	4.4
Fabricated Parts	56.1	5.4	21.3	12.5	4.6
Chemicals	58.6	7.1	16.3	16.5	1.4
Raw Materials	84.2	5.7	4.3	4.3	1.4
AGRICULTURAL:					
Durables	48.7	7.5	30.6	11.9	.6
Nondurables	40.5	4.4	37.2	17.7	—
CONSUMER:					
Durables	44.3	8.3	27.7	16.5	3.1
Petroleum Products	75.5	4.4	10.3	4.4	5.3
Chemicals (drugs)	43.3	15.0	20.0	20.4	1.3
Food, Liquor & Tobacco	39.0	16.3	29.2	15.3	.2
Other Nondurables	32.5	10.0	40.0	16.1	1.4

*The total points allocated to the five approaches to pricing sometimes equal slightly less than 100 because of rounding or because some other approach was given by a respondent.

the minds of consumers.

Cost-plus, or standard cost, pricing received its greatest emphasis among manufacturers of capital goods, agricultural durables and nondurables, and consumer nondurables other than food, liquor, tobacco, and drugs.

Pricing according to what the market will bear was most important to producers of consumer chemicals (20.4 points). This strategy was also relatively important among those marketing industrial chemicals, agricultural nondurables, consumer durables, and consumer nondurables.

Pricing according to government rules and regulations was about the least important strategy for all industries other than the aerospace and defense contractors.

[112]

Pricing Strategy And The Product-Market

Unlike the hypotheses concerning the relation of product effort and sales effort to the sophistication of the product-market, we assume no such relationship exists for pricing strategy. Statistically stated, our only hypothesis concerning pricing strategy is that pricing strategy is not significantly related to the nature of the product-market.

The average importance of pricing strategy associated with each level of each product-market attribute is shown in Table VIII-4.

Table VIII–4

AVERAGE POINT ALLOCATIONS TO PRICING CLASSIFIED ACCORDING TO PRODUCT-MARKET ATTRIBUTE LEVELS

Product-Market Attributes	Product-Market Attribute Levels				
	1	2	3	4&5	F**
Product Complexity	19.5	18.5	16.9	16.8	.10139
(N)*	(202)	(122)	(91)	(65)	
Buying Motives	18.8	17.9	18.8	13.1	.12076
(N)	(335)	(81)	(40)	(24)	
Buyer Effort	19.9	18.5	18.0	16.3	.12207
(N)	(146)	(118)	(118)	(97)	
Level of Comprehension	19.1	17.2	17.2	20.0	.12917
(N)	(256)	(99)	(96)	(29)	

Note: *N is the number of observations for each level of each product-market attribute.

 **F values of 2.39 or larger are statistically significant at the .05 level. The F values apply to the differences among the means and are obtained by an analysis of variance test.

There appears to be a slight positive relationship between the importance attributed to pricing and product complexity. The average number of points allocated to pricing varied from 16.8 among those with the least sophisticated products (levels four and five) to 19.5 among those with the most sophisticated products (level one). Similarly, there is a positive relationship between the perceived importance of pricing and amount of buyer effort. In other words, pricing is generally considered most important when buyer effort is great and product complexity is high. However, the differences among the average point allocations are not statistically significant.

For each of the product-market attributes, there is no statistically significant relationship between the perceived importance of pricing and the measures of the attributes. Therefore, the hypothesis is supported that the importance of pricing is not significantly related to the nature of the product-market. However, there is some evidence to suggest a slight tendency for pricing to be most important when product complexity and buyer effort are great.

Summary

The overall importance of pricing in the marketing strategies of U. S. manufacturers apparently does not vary dramatically from one industry to another. Furthermore, the share of market enjoyed by the firms, or their sales volume, did not significantly affect the perceived importance of pricing. However, the relative importance of specific approaches to price determination did vary considerably among the 13 major industries.

As for the totality of American industry, it appears that pricing according to competitive levels is by far the most important approach to price determination. Cost-plus, or standard cost, pricing was perceived as second in importance. Pricing according to what the market will bear was of lesser, but significant, importance. With the exception of the aerospace and defense manufacturers, government rules and regulations did not play a major role in price determination.

CHAPTER IX

THE INFLUENCE OF MARKET STRUCTURE ON COMPETITIVE STRATEGY

According to economic theory, market structure has an impact on pricing behavior. While various attempts have been made to relate non-price competitive behavior to the structural characteristics of an industry, success has been very limited.

It has been demonstrated that the emphasis placed on the various elements of competitive strategy varies considerably, depending upon the sophistication of the product-market. The purpose of this chapter is to examine possible relationships between marketing strategy and the size of company, share of market, and marketing costs. With or without any such relationships, the reader should find the marketing cost information of particular interest because so little data is available on this important aspect of corporate management.

The first and second parts of the chapter briefly examine the relationship between the perceived importance of the four major facets of competitive strategy and the sales volume and market share of the product. The third part examines marketing costs and includes information on the costs of several industries.

Marketing Strategy And Sales Volume

Table IX-1 presents the perceived importance of product effort classified according to the sales volume of the product. For example, 42.9 percent of all firms with product sales of less than $500,000 allocated 10 to 20 percent of their total strategy points to product effort. Among the firms with large sales

[115]

volumes ($10,000,000 or more), only 23.7 percent allocated less than 20 percent of their points to product effort. As the distribution and medians of Table IX-1 suggest, there is a slight positive relationship between sales volume and the perceived importance of the product facet of marketing strategy. In other words, large firms tended to place the most emphasis on product effort. The median respondent with product sales of $10,000,000 or more allocated 30 of his strategy points to product effort, while the median firm with product sales of $500,000 or less allocated 25 of its total strategy points to the product facet of competitive strategy.

Table IX–1

PRODUCT EFFORT AND SALES VOLUME

Sales Volume	Less than 10%	10% to 20%	20% to 30%	30% to 40%	40% to 50%	50% or more	Median Perceived Importance of Product Effort
Less than $500,000	—	42.9	14.3	21.4	21.4	—	25
$500,000 to $1,000,000	—	21.4	42.9	7.1	7.1	21.4	27
$1,000,000 to $10,000,000	8.3	18.9	32.6	14.4	15.9	9.9	27
$10,000,000 or more	7.3	16.4	25.2	24.6	14.2	12.3	30
All Firms	7.4	17.7	27.5	21.4	14.4	11.7	29

Percent of Firms with Perceived Importance of Product Effort of:

The relationship of sales effort to the sales volume of the product is pictured in Table IX-2. While the relationship is weak, the medians indicate that firms with product sales of $10,000,000 or more place less emphasis on marketing communication than companies with a lesser sales volume. Also, no firm with product sales of less than $1,000,000 allocated fewer than 20 percent of the total strategy points to sales effort. In each of the four sales volume categories, the median firm attributed over 40 points to sales effort.

There is no observable relationship between sales volume and the perceived importance of distribution. As shown in Table IX-3, the medians of the four sales categories ranged from 11 to 15 points, with the smallest and largest firms having the higher

Table IX–2

SALES EFFORT AND SALES VOLUME

Percent of Firms with Perceived
Importance of Sales Effort of:

Sales Volume	Less than 10%	10% to 20%	20% to 30%	30% to 40%	40% to 50%	50% to 60%	60% to 70%	70% or more	Median Perceived Importance of Sales Effort
Less than $500,000	—	—	7.1	28.6	21.4	7.1	28.6	7.1	47
$500,000 to $1,000,000	—	—	28.6	14.3	14.3	42.9	—	—	45
$1,000,000 to $10,000,000	1.5	1.5	17.4	14.4	22.0	24.2	7.6	11.4	47
$10,000,000 or more	1.3	4.4	15.8	24.6	22.7	16.1	6.3	8.8	42
All Firms	1.2	3.3	16.6	21.8	22.0	18.5	7.4	9.2	43

medians. The small differences involved could easily be due to chance, rather than any real difference in the perceived importance of distribution that is associated with sales volume.

Table IX–3

DISTRIBUTION AND SALES VOLUME

Percent of Firms with Perceived
Importance of Distribution of:

Sales Volume	Less than 10%	10% to 20%	20% to 30%	30% or more	Median Perceived Importance of Distribution
Less than $500,000	28.6	50.0	7.1	14.3	14
$500,000 to $1,000,000	35.7	42.9	14.3	7.1	13
$1,000,000 to $10,000,000	46.2	28.8	19.7	5.3	11
$10,000,000 or more	34.4	32.8	24.3	8.5	15
All Firms	37.6	32.7	22.2	7.6	14

The medians in Table IX-4 indicate that there is little difference in the perceived importance of pricing among firms with various sales volumes. However, the percentage distribution does indicate one difference; no firm with a product having sales of less than $500,000 allocated 30 or more of the total strategy points to pricing. In other words, there appears to be a tendency for small firms to place less emphasis on pricing than the larger firms.

[117]

Table IX–4

PRICING AND SALES VOLUME

	Percent of Firms with Perceived Importance of Pricing of:						
Sales Volume	Less than 10%	10% to 20%	20% to 30%	30% to 40%	40% to 50%	50% or more	Median Perceived Importance of Pricing
Less than $500,000	7.1	42.9	50.0	—	—	—	20
$500,000 to $1,000,000	—	42.9	50.0	7.1	—	—	21
$1,000,000 to $10,000,000	20.5	23.5	34.1	10.6	6.8	4.6	22
$10,000,000 or more	18.6	29.7	34.1	12.0	3.5	2.2	20
All Firms	18.3	28.3	35.1	11.3	4.3	2.7	21

In summary, the perceived importance of the various facets of competitive strategy varied slightly with the sales volume of the product. The product and pricing facets tended to be slightly more important among the larger firms, while sales volume was slightly more important among the companies with a relatively small volume of product sales. However, the relationships involved were not nearly as strong as those associated with the characteristics of the product-market.[1]

In other words, the characteristics of the product-market are superior to sales volume in explaining the differences in the marketing strategies of various companies.

Marketing Strategy And Market Share

While the perceived importance of the various facets of competitive strategy and market share were not highly correlated, there was a tendency for the importance of product effort to vary directly with share of market. As shown in Table IX-5, the median company among those with products having a less than five percent share of market allocated 24 points to product effort. On the other hand, the median company among those having the largest share of market (45 percent or more) allocated 37 points to product effort. Apparently, the larger firms within an industry usually place the greatest emphasis on the

---

[1] While the data do not meet the requirements for correlation and regression analyses, such analyses were made. The relationships between strategy and product-market were substantially stronger than those between strategy and sales volume.

product facet of competitive strategy. However, share of market was less important than the characteristics of the product-market in explaining the varying degrees of emphasis placed on product effort.

Table IX-5

PRODUCT EFFORT AND MARKET SHARE

	Percent of Firms with Perceived Importance of Product Effort of:						
Share of Market	Less than 10%	10% to 20%	20% to 30%	30% to 40%	40% to 50%	50% or more	Median Importance of Product Effort
Less than 5%	12.2	24.5	30.6	8.2	14.3	10.2	24
5% to 15%	8.7	23.5	27.0	20.9	14.8	5.2	27
15% to 25%	7.5	22.3	26.6	25.5	12.8	5.3	28
25% to 35%	4.7	18.8	29.4	20.0	11.8	15.3	29
35% to 45%	2.2	4.4	32.6	28.3	17.4	15.2	34
45% or more	8.2	8.2	15.1	24.7	19.2	24.7	37
All Firms	7.4	17.7	27.5	21.4	14.4	11.7	29

The perceived importance of sales effort, as related to market share, is shown in Table IX-6. As indicated, there was a slight negative relationship between the emphasis placed on sales effort and the product's share of market. However, the correlation was weak and was due to the unusually large emphasis placed on sales

Table IX-6

SALES EFFORT AND MARKET SHARE

	Percent of Firms with Perceived Importance of Sales Effort of:						
Share of Market	Less than 10%	10% to 20%	20% to 30%	30% to 40%	40% to 50%	50% or more	Median Importance of Sales Effort
Less than 5%	2.0	2.0	10.2	10.2	16.3	59.2	58
5% to 15%	.9	4.4	16.5	17.4	27.8	33.1	44
15% to 25%	2.1	2.1	13.8	23.4	19.2	39.4	44
25% to 35%	1.2	4.7	12.9	25.9	18.8	36.5	42
35% to 45%	—	4.4	21.7	28.3	26.1	19.6	38
45% or more	—	1.4	16.4	26.0	26.0	30.1	42
All Firms	1.2	3.3	16.6	21.8	22.0	35.1	43

effort by those companies having a less than five percent share of market. For example, 59 percent of all such firms allocated 50 or more points to sales effort. The median allocation of all companies with a less than five percent share of market was 58 points; the medians for the other groups of firms ranged from 38 to 44.

The perceived importance of distribution and share of market were also negatively related, but the relationship was weak. As indicated by the medians in Table IX-7, those firms with products having a share of market of less than 25 percent generally placed greater emphasis on distribution than the companies enjoying a share of market of 25 percent or more. However, the difference is small and share of market is not particularly useful in explaining the variation in the emphasis placed on distribution.

Table IX–7

DISTRIBUTION AND MARKET SHARE

Share of Market	Percent of Firms with Perceived Importance of Distribution of:						
	Less than 10%	10% to 20%	20% to 30%	30% to 40%	40% to 50%	50% or more	Median Importance of Distribution
Less than 5%	49.0	16.3	26.5	4.1	4.1	—	11
5% to 15%	32.2	37.4	21.7	5.2	—	3.5	15
15% to 25%	31.9	31.9	23.4	7.5	5.3	—	16
25% to 35%	29.4	41.2	23.5	4.7	1.2	—	13
35% to 45%	41.3	32.6	21.7	2.2	—	2.2	13
45% or more	54.8	30.1	11.0	2.7	—	1.4	9
All Firms	37.6	32.7	22.2	4.7	1.6	1.2	14

The perceived importance of pricing was also inversely related to share of market. However, the relationship was weak, being primarily due to the less-than-average emphasis placed on pricing by companies having small market shares. As shown in Table IX-8, the median of those with less than five percent of the market allocated only 16 points to pricing. The typical firm with five percent or more of the market allocated 21 points to pricing.

Table IX–8

PRICING AND MARKET SHARE

Percent of Firms with Perceived
Importance of Pricing of:

Share of Market	Less than 10%	10% to 20%	20% to 30%	30% to 40%	40% to 50%	50% or more	Median Importance of Pricing
Less than 5%	32.7	28.6	30.6	4.1	—	4.1	16
5% to 15%	15.7	29.6	33.9	11.3	6.1	3.5	21
15% to 25%	16.0	30.9	31.9	10.6	7.5	3.2	21
25% to 35%	16.5	32.9	40.0	8.2	1.2	1.2	20
35% to 45%	10.9	26.1	39.1	19.6	—	4.3	23
45% or more	21.9	26.0	30.1	16.4	4.1	1.4	21
All Firms	18.3	28.3	35.1	11.3	4.3	2.7	21

Marketing Strategy And Marketing Costs

Is the nature or composition of the marketing strategy related to marketing costs? To provide an insight into this question, the allocations to the various components of marketing strategy are cross-classified with the percent of total costs that are marketing costs.

As shown in Table IX-9, the marketing costs of the respondents ranged from less than five percent to over 30 percent of total costs. However, the emphasis placed on product effort did not differ significantly among the various marketing cost categories. For example, products with marketing costs of less than five percent, five to 10 percent, and 20 to 25 percent all had a median of 30 strategy points allocated to product effort. However, there was a slight tendency for firms with marketing costs of over 25 percent to place somewhat greater emphasis on product effort. Perhaps it would be more reasonable to conclude that firms with a great emphasis on product effort tended to have higher marketing costs. However, the differences involved are not large and may be more random than real.

As shown in Table IX-10, the perceived relative importance of sales effort was not rigorously related to marketing costs. However, firms with marketing costs of 25 percent or more tended to place slightly less emphasis on sales effort. For exam-

Table IX–9

PRODUCT EFFORT AND MARKETING COSTS[1]

Percent of Firms with Perceived
Importance of Product Effort of:

Marketing Costs	Less than 10%	10% to 20%	20% to 30%	30% to 40%	40% to 50%	50% or more	Median Perceived Importance of Product Effort
Less than 5%	13.1	13.1	24.2	16.2	16.2	17.2	30
5% to 10%	4.7	19.4	25.6	24.8	10.9	14.7	30
10% to 15%	4.7	18.8	32.9	21.2	12.9	9.4	28
15% to 20%	13.6	27.3	31.8	11.4	11.4	4.5	23
20% to 25%	—	15.6	33.3	28.9	22.2	—	30
25% to 30%	5.9	17.7	17.7	35.3	17.7	5.9	32
30% or more	5.1	25.6	18.0	18.0	18.0	15.4	31
All Firms	7.4	17.7	27.5	21.4	14.4	11.7	29

[1] Marketing costs as a percent of total costs. The total for each row may not equal 100 percent because some respondents did not report their marketing costs.

ple, while the median company among all firms allocated 43 points to sales effort, the median firm with marketing costs of 25 to 30 percent allocated 37 points to sales effort.

There was a slight tendency for marketing costs and the perceived importance of distribution to be positively related. As shown in Table IX-11, firms with marketing costs of less than five percent had a median allocation of nine points to distribution. On the other hand, the median allocation of firms with marketing costs of over 25 percent was 16.

The perceived importance of pricing and marketing costs tended to be inversely related. In other words, firms with marketing costs of less than 15 percent were the most prone to emphasize pricing in their competitive strategy. As shown in Table IX-12, however, the differences among the median point allocations to pricing did not vary markedly from one cost category to another.

In summary, firms having relatively low marketing costs tended to place more emphasis on pricing and sales effort than other companies. Conversely, firms having relatively high marketing costs tended to allocate more points to product effort and distribution.

Table IX–10

SALES EFFORT AND MARKETING COSTS[1]

Percent of Firms with Perceived
Importance of Sales Effort:

Marketing Costs	Less than 10%	10% to 20%	20% to 30%	30% to 40%	40% to 50%	50% to 60%	60% to 70%	70% or more	Median Perceived Importance of Sales Effort
Less than 5%	4.0	8.1	17.2	16.2	20.2	20.2	2.0	12.1	43
5% to 10%	—	3.1	14.7	27.1	22.5	15.5	7.0	10.1	42
10% to 15%	—	2.4	16.5	18.8	27.1	23.5	7.1	4.7	45
15% to 20%	—	—	9.1	13.6	20.5	22.7	13.6	20.5	53
20% to 25%	—	—	11.1	26.7	26.7	17.8	11.1	6.7	45
25% to 30%	—	—	29.4	29.4	23.5	5.9	5.9	5.9	37
30% or more	—	2.6	18.0	30.8	12.8	15.4	12.8	7.7	40
All firms	1.2	3.3	16.6	21.8	22.0	18.5	7.4	9.2	43

[1] Marketing costs as a percent of total costs. The total for each row may not equal 100% because some respondents did not report their marketing costs.

Table IX–11

DISTRIBUTION AND MARKETING COSTS[1]

Percent of Firms with Perceived
Importance of Distribution:

Marketing Costs	Less than 10%	10% to 20%	20% to 30%	30% to 40%	40% or more	Median Perceived Importance of Distribution
Less than 5%	56.6	21.2	17.2	4.0	1.0	9
5% to 10%	34.9	32.6	21.7	7.0	3.9	15
10% to 15%	32.9	35.3	27.1	1.2	3.5	15
15% to 20%	36.4	40.9	15.9	4.6	2.3	13
20% to 25%	35.6	33.3	22.2	8.9	——	14
25% to 30%	23.5	41.2	17.7	5.9	11.8	16
30% or more	23.1	43.6	25.6	5.1	2.6	16
All firms	37.6	32.7	22.2	4.7	2.9	14

[1] Marketing costs as a percent of total costs. The total for each row may not equal 100% because some respondents did not report their marketing costs.

Table IX–12

PRICING AND MARKETING COSTS[1]

Percent of Firms with Perceived
Importance of Pricing of:

Marketing Costs	Less than 10%	10% to 20%	20% to 30%	30% to 40%	40% to 50%	50% or more	Median Perceived Importance of Pricing
Less than 5%	24.2	17.2	32.3	14.1	3.0	9.1	23
5% to 10%	20.9	26.4	31.8	14.0	5.4	1.6	21
10% to 15%	15.3	22.4	45.9	9.4	4.7	2.4	23
15% to 20%	20.5	40.9	27.3	6.8	4.6	——	17
20% to 25%	8.9	37.8	33.3	17.8	2.2	——	21
25% to 30%	——	52.9	47.1	——	——	——	19
30% or more	15.4	43.6	33.3	5.1	2.6	——	18
All firms	18.3	28.3	35.1	11.3	4.3	2.7	21

[1] Marketing costs as a percent of total costs. The total for each row may not equal 100% because some respondents did not report their marketing costs.

Sales Volume And Marketing Costs

Marketing costs did vary markedly with the sales volume of the product. As shown in Table IX-13, the median marketing cost for all products included in the survey was 10 percent. However, products with sales of $10,000,000 or more had a median

cost of only 8 percent, while those with sales of less than $500,000 had median marketing costs of 23 percent. In other words, marketing costs varied inversely with the sales volume of the product. Without considering other factors, one would conclude that there appear to be distinct economies of large scale in the marketing of manufactured goods.

Table IX–13
SALES VOLUME AND MARKETING COSTS[1]

	Percent of Firms with Marketing Costs of:					
Sales Volume of Product	Less than 5%	5% to 10%	10% to 20%	20% to 30%	30% or more	Median Marketing Costs
Less than $500,000	7.1	7.1	28.6	28.6	28.6	23
$500,000 to $1,000,000	14.3	14.3	21.4	28.6	21.4	20
$1,000,000 to $10,000,000	11.4	29.6	38.7	14.4	3.8	12
$10,000,000 or more	25.2	27.4	22.1	10.7	8.5	8
All firms	20.3	26.5	26.5	12.7	8.0	10

[1] Marketing costs as a percent of total costs. The total for each row may not equal 100% because some respondents did not report their marketing costs.

Market Share And Marketing Costs

Contrary to what one might expect given the distinct inverse relationship between marketing costs and sales volume, there was only a slight relationship between costs and market share (see Table IX-14). The typical firm having a product with less than

Table IX–14
SHARE OF MARKET AND MARKETING COSTS[1]

	Percent of Products with Marketing Costs of:					
Share of Market	Less than 5%	5% to 10%	10% to 20%	20% to 30%	30% or more	Median Marketing Costs
Less than 5%	32.7	14.3	26.5	16.3	10.2	11
5% to 15%	17.4	26.1	27.8	13.9	12.2	12
15% to 25%	16.0	29.8	31.9	12.8	6.4	11
25% to 35%	23.5	30.6	27.0	13.0	4.7	9
35% to 45%	23.9	28.3	28.3	8.7	10.9	10
45% or more	20.6	30.1	23.3	13.7	6.9	9
All firms	20.3	26.5	26.5	12.7	8.0	10

[1] Marketing costs as a percent of total costs. The total for each row may not equal 100% because some respondents did not report their marketing costs.

25 percent of the market had marketing costs of 11 percent; the typical firm enjoying a share of market of 25 percent or more had marketing costs of 9 percent. Given the much larger range of marketing costs associated with sales volume, it appears that the small differences associated with market share are likely to be due to differences in sales volume. Stated somewhat differently, there apparently is little, if any, marketing cost advantage associated with share of market or degree of monopolistic power.

Marketing Costs Of Various Industries

There were distinct differences in the marketing costs of various industries. For example, 58 percent of the firms in the aerospace and defense industry had marketing costs of less than 5 percent, while only 6 percent of the consumer durable producers had marketing costs that low. The median marketing costs were lowest in the aerospace and defense and raw material industries, 4 and 6 percent respectively. Among the industrial goods producers, the median marketing costs of capital goods producers was the highest—10 percent. Both agricultural goods and construction equipment had median costs of 11 percent.

As shown in Table IX-15, the highest marketing costs occurred in the consumer nondurable goods industries. Twenty-five percent of the products in this group had marketing costs of 30 percent or more. The median marketing costs for the nondurable goods producers was 20 percent.

Given their distribution, one could hypothesize that marketing costs, as a percent of total costs, tend to vary inversely with the sophistication of the product-market. In any event, marketing costs are largest among manufacturers of consumer nondurables and least among producers of industrial goods. Given the fact that the latter have fewer customers to reach, one would expect less need for expenditures on mass communications and distribution and, therefore, a lower level of expenditures. On the other hand, consumer goods producers pass on many of their communication and distribution functions to the channel of distribution. Despite their greater utilization of channels, they generally have the highest marketing costs.

Table IX–15

MARKETING COSTS IN VARIOUS INDUSTRIES

Industries	Percent of Products with Marketing Costs of:							
	Less than 5%	5% to 10%	10% to 15%	15% to 20%	20% to 25%	25% to 30%	30% or more	Median Marketing Costs
Aerospace & Defense	58.1	16.1	9.7	3.2	9.7	——	3.2	4
Raw Materials	43.8	25.0	18.8	12.5	——	——	——	6
Industrial Chemicals	33.3	38.1	16.7	2.4	4.8	2.4	2.4	7
Fabricated Parts and Materials	23.4	39.1	17.2	6.3	8.7	2.3	3.1	8
Capital Goods	20.9	29.6	19.8	7.4	12.3	3.7	6.2	10
Agricultural Goods	4.0	36.0	32.0	12.0	8.0	4.0	4.0	11
Construction Equipment	13.0	30.4	21.7	21.7	8.7	——	4.3	11
Consumer Durables	5.6	33.3	22.2	16.7	——	11.1	11.1	12
Consumer Nondurables	10.3	9.2	19.5	13.8	14.9	6.9	25.3	20

Conclusion

Small differences, if any, can be found in the emphasis placed on the major facets of competitive strategy among producers of various sizes, share of market, and marketing costs. The differences that do exist are considerably smaller than those associated with the sophistication of the product-market.

Distinct differences exist in the marketing costs of various industries, with costs tending to vary inversely with the sophistication of the product-market. Median marketing costs ranged from 4 percent among aerospace and defense contractors to 20 percent among producers of consumer nondurable goods. About equally large differences occurred among products with various levels of sales. Products having sales of less than $500,000 had median marketing costs of 23 percent, while those with sales of over $10,000,000 had median costs of only 8 percent. There was little relationship between marketing costs and share of market. The median marketing costs of all firms was 10 percent.

CHAPTER X

CONCLUSION AND APPLICATION

While price, product and sales efforts are all indispensible and vitally important elements of marketing mix, the nonprice elements are of major significance in the strategies of modern industry. There appears to be, at most, only a slight relationship between the importance of the nonprice elements and the size and market share of a company. On the other hand, there is a definite relationship between the perceived importance of product and sales efforts facets and the behavioral characteristics of the product-market.

More specifically, the relative importance of product effort varies directly with the purchasing efforts and knowledge of the buyer, the technical nature of the product, and the strength of operational buying motives. The significance of sales effort in the marketing mix varies inversely with the technical nature of the product, purchasing efforts and knowledge of the buyer, while varying directly with the strength of socio-psychological buying motives.

Although the above conceptual guidelines are general in nature, they are capable of explaining many of the differences in the marketing strategies of a wide range of successful products in American industry.

Applying The Concepts Of The Product-Market

The product-market model should be useful in evaluating current strategies and in planning improved marketing programs for the future. One approach is to compare the current strategy for

a product to that used by the responding producers with similar products. This should be especially useful to the industrial goods manufacturer because industrial goods were well represented in the study.

To make this comparison, the reader should, for each selected product, complete the product-market questionnaire which appears in Appendix II. Upon doing this, one can compare his point allocations to product effort, pricing, sales effort and distribution to those of similar manufacturers participating in the study. One may also wish to compare his allocations to the specific elements of each major facet to those of the responding companies.

The difference between one's allocations and those of the respondents may indicate the direction of desirable change. For example, suppose one has allocated 20 points to product effort while similar manufacturers allocated 38 points to that facet. Perhaps the effectiveness of one's marketing program could be improved by placing greater emphasis on the product facet. To obtain more specific guidance, one may compare point allocations to technical R & D, pre- and postsale product service, marketing research relating to product development, and fashion R & D.

While the above exercise may be of value, the greatest potential benefit of the product-market model lies in its philosophical implications. *To design efficient and effective marketing strategies, management must create marketing programs that are consonant or in harmony with the nature of the product and, more important, the behavioral characteristics of the market for that product.* Not only should the knowledge, purchasing efforts and motivation of the buyer be considered, but so should any other dominant behavioral characteristic.

The usefulness of this philosophical approach goes beyond selecting an appropriate balance of product effort and sales effort. For example, suppose one is concerned with the question of distribution—how much reliance should be placed on middlemen, as opposed to selling direct, and how intensive should the distribution be? If the product involved is a low-priced convenience good without strong brand loyalty, such as a flashlight battery, then consumers will purchase the product with a minimum of effort. This is not to imply that the consumer may not have a

brand preference, such as Ray-O-Vac or Eveready; however, the consumer is unlikely to go to a second store to obtain the preferred brand if it is not available at the first retail unit visited.

The implication of this pattern of purchasing behavior is that flashlight batteries, and other convenience goods without strong brand loyalty, should have the greatest distribution possible. The marketing program should seek to obtain as many distribution outlets as is economically possible, and should even attempt to get the product in several departments of a large retail unit. Product development may be required to accomplish this. For example, Ray-O-Vac has developed sportsman batteries, camera batteries, and several other versions of the dry cell. Consequently, one can find Ray-O-Vac batteries in the hardware, sporting goods, toy, camera, and other departments of many retail stores. In any event, many retail outlets and, therefore, an extensive use of middlemen, are needed to obtain large sales of a convenience good and *it is the behavioral characteristics of the buyer that dictate this strategy.*

Changing The Marketing Program

If a company has experienced reasonable success through its current marketing program, it is likely to be reluctant to change that program dramatically, even though an analysis of the product-market suggests a different balance of product effort and sales effort. Suppose, for example, that the analysis indicates that greater sales or the same sales with lower marketing costs could be obtained by shifting emphasis from sales effort to product effort. Being cautious, management does not wish to assume the risk of a sudden and substantial change in the company's marketing strategy. However, one segment of the firm's market is selected as a test area and advertising is discontinued in a medium which is distributed in that area. Concurrently, a service engineer is added to the staff in the test area. The salary and expenses of the service engineer are about 50 percent of the cost of the discontinued advertisement. The service engineer devotes his efforts to providing additional service to existing customers and presale service for potential customers.

Nine months elapse and sales in the test area have risen five percent more than in other similar market areas of the company. Management can find no external event within the test area to

account for the greater rise of sales. On the basis of the sales increase and the decrease of marketing expenditures, management has evidence that greater sales can be obtained at less expense by using the strategy indicated by the product-market analysis. Accordingly, the company's marketing strategy is revised in other market areas and management continues to test the shifting of emphasis from sales effort to product effort.

The purpose of this illustration is to suggest how management might utilize experimentation and the product-market model to move toward an optimum nonprice competitive strategy.

The Formulation Of Marketing Strategies

The question arises, does business management currently use some informal approximation of the product-market model? Certainly much of the data from the 485 product strategies included in the analysis conformed to the model.

Through past experience and the process of trial and error, successful managements may have arrived at a combination of product and sales efforts which works well without a conscious awareness of the product-market characteristics and their relationship to marketing strategy. In some companies, however, the competitive strategy is the result of a conscious analysis of the behavioral characteristics of the market. The Ray-O-Vac and Wilson Products Divisions of ESB Corporation provide an illustration.

Owen R. Slauson, President of the Ray-O-Vac Division, was asked to outline his marketing strategy for flashlight batteries and industrial safety equipment.[1] Without any introduction or information concerning the product-market model (which might have biased the response), Mr. Slauson provided a lengthy description of the marketing strategies for the two products. *The strategies were very different and each was predicated on a careful and detailed analysis of the products and their customers.* To quote Mr. Slauson as he summarized his philosophy of marketing

---

[1] At the time of the interview, Mr. Slauson was Vice-President for Domestic Sales and directed the marketing programs for both the Ray-O-Vac and Wilson Products Divisions of ESB.

[132]

management, "The differences in our merchandising policies are dictated by the differences in the products and the differences in their markets. It is the product, the type of people using it, and how it is purchased and used that determines our merchandising policy. It couldn't be any other way."

The letters accompanying several responses also stated a definite awareness of the product and the customer in formulating competitive strategy. Whether it is by a successful process of trial and error or conscious management effort, it may be concluded that many successful companies do select nonprice competitive strategies that conform to the product-market decision model.

PEDAGOGICAL APPROACH TO THE OPTIMUM COMPETITIVE STRATEGY

The optimum combination of price and nonprice competitive tactics (from the firm's point of view) may be pedagogically derived by a simple and realistic two-stage approach. This approach places *no* restrictions on the shape of product cost curves[1] and is capable of handling the desire for both security and short-run profits. Most important of all, the analysis emphasizes the role of nonprice competitive tactics and their relationship to price.

Stage I—Equi-Marginal Returns From Sales And Product Expenditures

To maximize the returns from an expenditure, the entrepreneur should *seek to equate* the marginal sales productivities of the last dollar invested in product and sales effort. In other words, the marginal dollar (or more realistically, the marginal unit of dollars) spent on each type of competitive activity should yield an equal volume of sales. Symbolically, letting S represent the increase in sales resulting from ME, the marginal unit of expenditure, the following equation represents the optimum combination of product and sales efforts.

$$\frac{S_1}{ME_1} = \frac{S_2}{ME_2}$$

Subscript 1 denotes product effort and subscript 2 denotes sales effort.

Although marginal analysis is pedagogically useful in visualizing the optimum behavior of the firm, it is of questionable value

---

[1] A necessary condition to classical competitive analysis is the assumption of "U" shaped production cost curves. This assumption has frequently been challenged on the grounds that product cost curves are not always subject to decreasing returns. For a discussion of the shape of cost curves, see The American Economic Association, *Readings in Price Theory* (Homewood, Illinois: Richard D. Irwin, Inc., 1952), pp. 180-279.

to marketing management. The typical executive does not understand marginal analysis and, even if he did, could not determine the marginal returns from the last dollar spent on each marketing activity.

In the effort to overcome part of these difficulties, we shall use an approach which substitutes total expenditures for marginal expenditures—equal sales analysis.

Using a modification of the Hicksian indifference curve[2], the expenditures for all activities pertaining to the product facet

Figure I

THE EQUAL SALES CURVE

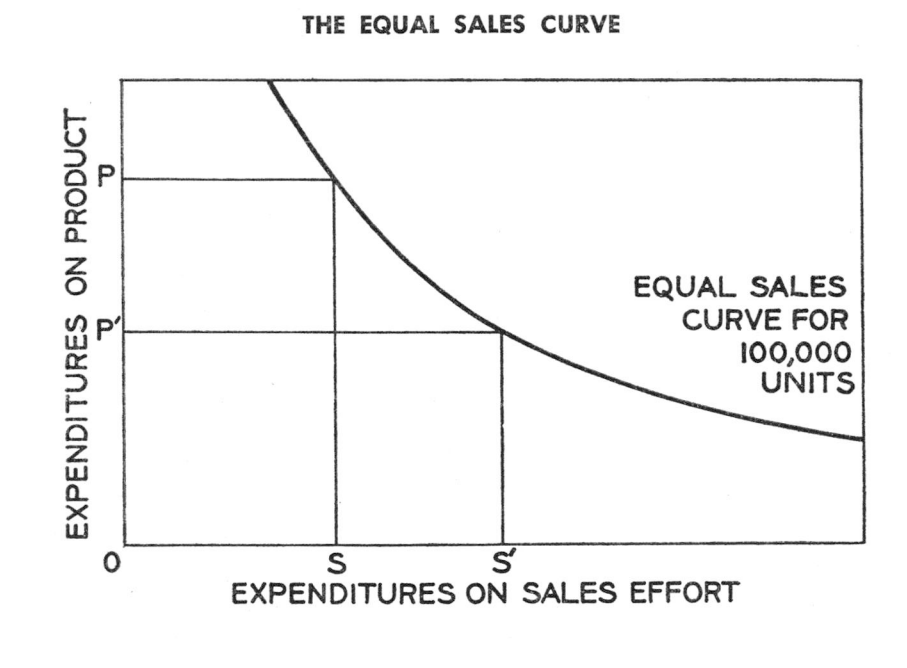

[2] A brief explanation of indifference curve analysis may be found in Alfred W. Stonier and Douglas C. Hague, *A Textbook of Economic Theory* (New York: Longmans Green and Co., 1956), pp. 43-76.

of competitive behavior are grouped on the Y axis, and the expenditures for sales efforts are grouped on the X axis, as shown in Figure 1. Assuming prices are constant, economic and competitive conditions are such that if OP dollars are expended on product (and service), and OS dollars are expended on sales effort, an estimated 100,000 units of the product will be sold. Again, if OP' is expended on product, and OS' on sales effort, an estimated 100,000 units will be sold. Similarly, the coordinates of all other points on the equal sales curve show the estimated combinations of product and sales effort that would produce a sales volume of 100,000 units.

Equal sales curves for other sales volumes may be drawn into the diagram to form an equal sales map, as shown in Figure 2. Before selecting the optimum combination of product and sales effort for any given expenditure, the probable shape of equal sales curves deserves comment. First, equal sales curves will slope downward and to the right. This will be the case so long as additional dollars expended on either facet of marketing effort do not produce negative sales. Although improbable, the latter might occur. For example, a manufacturer might spend so much on advertising that the public became tired of the product. However, this is quite unlikely as it would not be feasible for a firm to precipitate such a situation. An entrepreneur who is attempting to maximize profits or security would not knowingly use a combination of marketing factors on an upward-sloping portion of an equal sales curve. We can, therefore, ignore that possibility in the entrepreneur's planning. Similarly, a horizontal range of an equal sales curve, although it might exist, would never include a feasible operating strategy; the given sales volume could always be obtained with less expense. Therefore, we can assume that, over those ranges in which it would be practical to operate, equal sales curves slope downward to the right.

The second assumption about equal sales curves is that they are convex to the origin. This clearly implies something about the marginal significance of one facet in terms of the other. With equal sales curves the marginal significance of one facet, X, in terms of the other facet, Y, is the dollars of the facet Y which it is possible to give up in exchange for one more dollar of facet X without altering the amount of the product sold. The assumption that equal sales curves are convex to the origin im-

plies that the marginal significance of any one facet in terms of the other will always diminish along any equal sales curve. That is to say, the more that is expended on facet Y, the less it will be necessary to spend on facet X to maintain the same volume of sales. The convex assumption—that marginal significance always diminishes—can be justified in about the same way as the first assumption, the entrepreneur would not knowingly operate on a concave portion of an equal sales curve. Since the marginal significance of the facet he is purchasing is increasing, it would pay him to continue buying more of it until the equal sales curve becomes convex again and the marginal significance begins to decrease and finally falls below price.

The third assumption is that no two equal sales curves can ever cross each other. If they did, both curves would have a point in common, and this would imply that two volumes of sales would occur from one combination of product and sales effort. In addition, the crossing of the curves would contradict the definition of equal sales curves.

Let us return to the problem of obtaining the optimum combination of product and sales effort for any given expenditure. The optimum combination will be that combination of product and sales effort enabling the entrepreneur to reach the highest equal sales curve. This curve will be tangent to the marketing expenditures line which represents the various combinations of product and sales effort that may be purchased for a given expenditure. At the point of tangency the relative prices of product and sales effort equal the marginal sales productivities of one facet in terms of the other. The consequence is maximum sales from the marketing expenditure. The point of tangency in Figure II represents the optimum combination for a marketing expenditure of $100,000. Fifty thousand dollars of this money (OP) is expended on product and service, and $50,000 (OS) is expended on sales efforts. The result of this optimum combination is a sales volume of 200,000 units. By estimating a greater number of equal sales curves and marketing expenditure lines, a more detailed picture of the various expenditure and sales alternatives may be derived. Assuming that the firm wishes to

Figure II

OPTIMUM COMBINATION OF PRODUCT AND SALES EFFORT

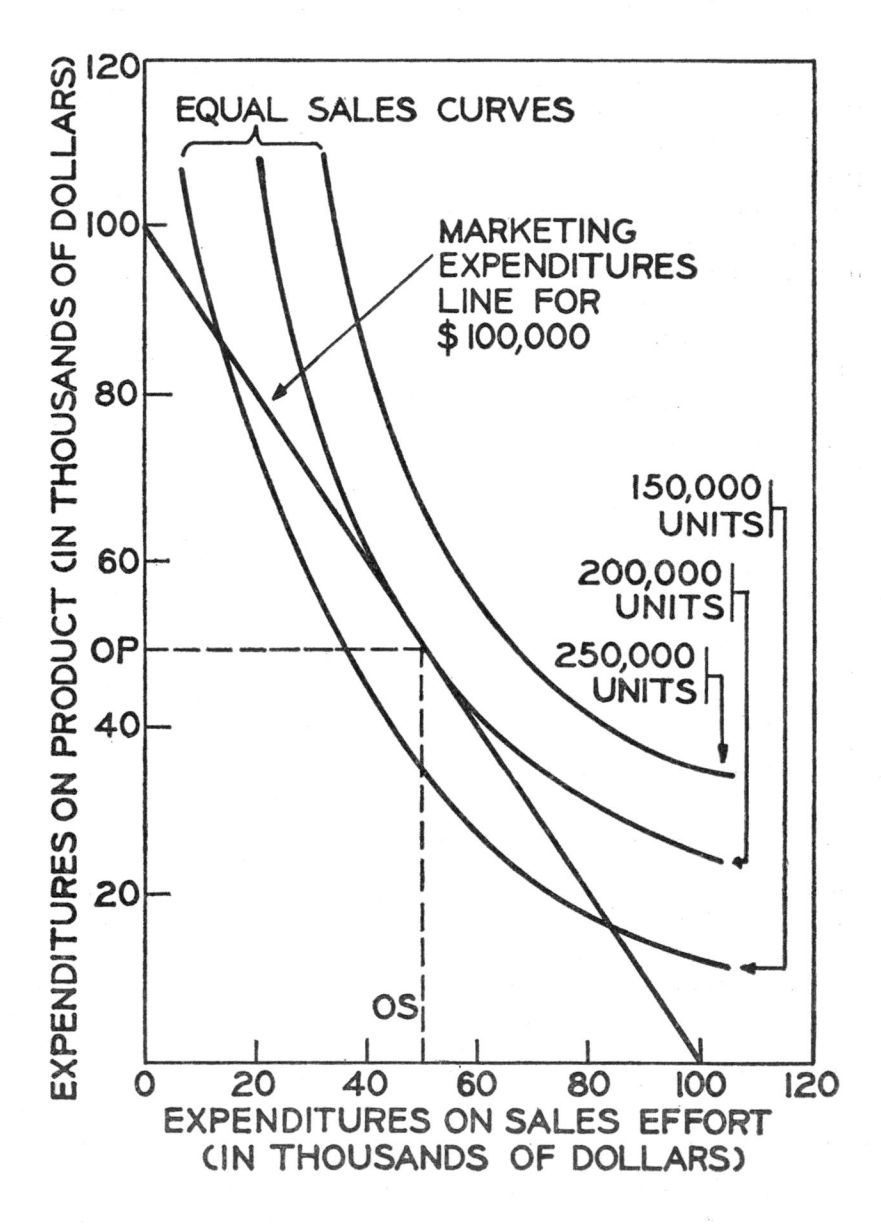

obtain a given sales volume as inexpensively as possible, or assuming that the firm desires the greatest sales volume possible from a given expenditure, an estimate of the optimum combination may be derived.

Although this approach entails a number of practical difficulties which would severely curtail its applicability, it provides an analytical framework within which to view the role of the nonprice parameters of competition. It shows that nonprice variables are just as capable of being theoretically formulated and theoretically solved as are the price variables with which economic theory has for so long been concerned. The analysis provides an indication of what must be done if solutions to marketing problems are to be scientifically derived. For example, the aforementioned solution of the optimum combination of product and sales effort (Figure II) revolves around the problem of identifying (or approximating) equal sales curves. If management could estimate the effect of the various elements of the marketing mix on sales volume, then management could determine:

1. A number of combinations of product and sales efforts that would yield a given sales volume, and

2. The combination of product and sales efforts that would yield maximum sales from a given expenditure.

The fact that the theoretical framework contains concepts which are not easily identified or quantified in practice—such as equal sales curves—is both a strength and a weakness. Its strength lies in the fact that the theoretical formulation is instructive because it pinpoints the problems that must be solved to reach optimality.

It is through the objective identification and, ultimately, the solution of such problems that marketing can, in practice, become a science. Hopefully, the product-market model will provide an approach for developing more efficient combinations of product and sales efforts.

Stage II—The Optimum Combination Of Price And Nonprice Competitive Tactics

By using the approach of Stage I, the optimum combination of nonprice facets for any given expenditure may be estimated. Stage I, however, fails to explain *how much* a firm should ex-

pend on marketing (product and sales effort), and what price should be charged.

To overcome these limitations, production costs and the range of feasible prices must be considered. There are usually only a few discrete prices available to the firm. For example, if a producer of notebook paper is currently charging twenty-five cents a pad, it would be foolish for him to consider a price of five cents (which would put him out of business because of losses), or a dollar (which would price him out of the market). The term *relevant prices* is useful in such a situation, and is defined as all possible prices which the firm might seriously consider. Therefore, if a manufacturer of fishing rods which are currently selling to wholesalers at $3.98 is estimating the profitability of charging $3.49, $3.98, or $4.49, the firm has only three relevant prices.

Given the present price of $3.98, the firm's production costs at various levels of output, and the minimum marketing expenditure necessary to obtain various sales volumes (i.e., the optimum combinations of marketing activities determined in Stage I), Figure III may be drawn. Given the various production and marketing costs and a price of $3.98 per unit, the firm shown in Figure III would maximize profits by selling 4,000 rods costing $8,000 to produce and $4,000 to market. The profit realized would be $3,920 ($3.98 x 4000 = $15,920 Total Revenue less $12,000 Total Costs = $3,920 Profit).

Before comparing this profit maximizing combination at the price of $3.98 to the optimum combinations of the other two relevant prices, Figure III is reconstructed as shown in Figure IV.

Figure IV simplifies Figure III by substituting Gross Profits for the difference between Total Revenue and Total Production Costs. Consequently, the role of marketing costs (TMC) is singled out and emphasized. In addition, an estimate of the firm's share of the market that each level of sales would represent is presented. This entrepreneur, in addition to making profits, may be concerned about security. The desire for security is frequently expressed in terms of:

1. A resistance to price change.
2. An attempt to obtain or maintain a certain share of the market.

Figure III
MAXIMIZING PROFITS

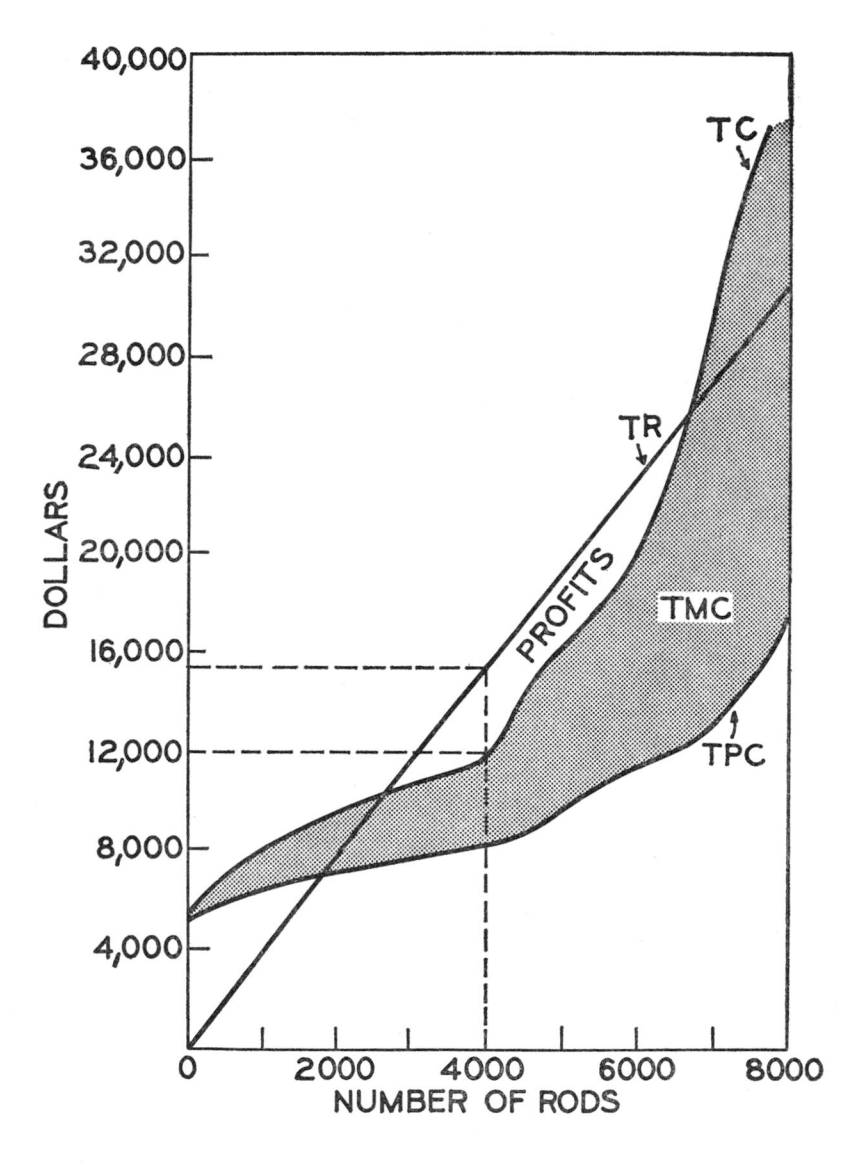

TPC = Total Production Costs for each level of output.

TMC = Total Marketing Costs necessary to sell each level of output (assuming a price of $3.98 and the use of an optimum combination of product and selling effort).

TC = Total Costs incurred in the production and marketing of each level of output.

TR = Total Revenue received from each level of sales.

If the first alternative is chosen, the firm will resist changing the price of its product, or it will charge the price established by the price leaders of the industry.[3] If this is the case, the manufacturer of fishing rods needs only to select the optimum combination of marketing expenditures that will maximize his profits at the established market price.

If the second alternative is selected, the entrepreneur will seek to use the combination of price, product, and sales efforts that will yield him a certain share of the market *with maximum profits attainable from that share.*

Assuming a price of $3.98, the producer of fishing rods can obtain anywhere from seven to 20 percent of the market and still operate at a profit. The entrepreneur may, out of a desire for a stronger position in the market, invest $6,500 in marketing and sell 5,000 rods to obtain a 15 percent share of the market and a profit of $3,200, rather than selling 4,000 rods with a maximum profit of $3,920 and only 12 percent of the market. Therefore, using the approach illustrated in Figures III and IV, both short-run profit and security may be considered simultaneously.

The entrepreneur has considered, to this point, the optimum competitive strategy at only one price. Assuming that management is willing to change price, other relevant prices are still to be evaluated. With only three discrete prices under considera-

---

[3] The price charged may be identical to, a certain amount less than, or a certain amount more than that of the price leader. However, the *relationship* of the firm's price to the price leader's price would remain constant.

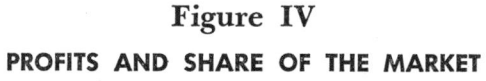

Figure IV
PROFITS AND SHARE OF THE MARKET

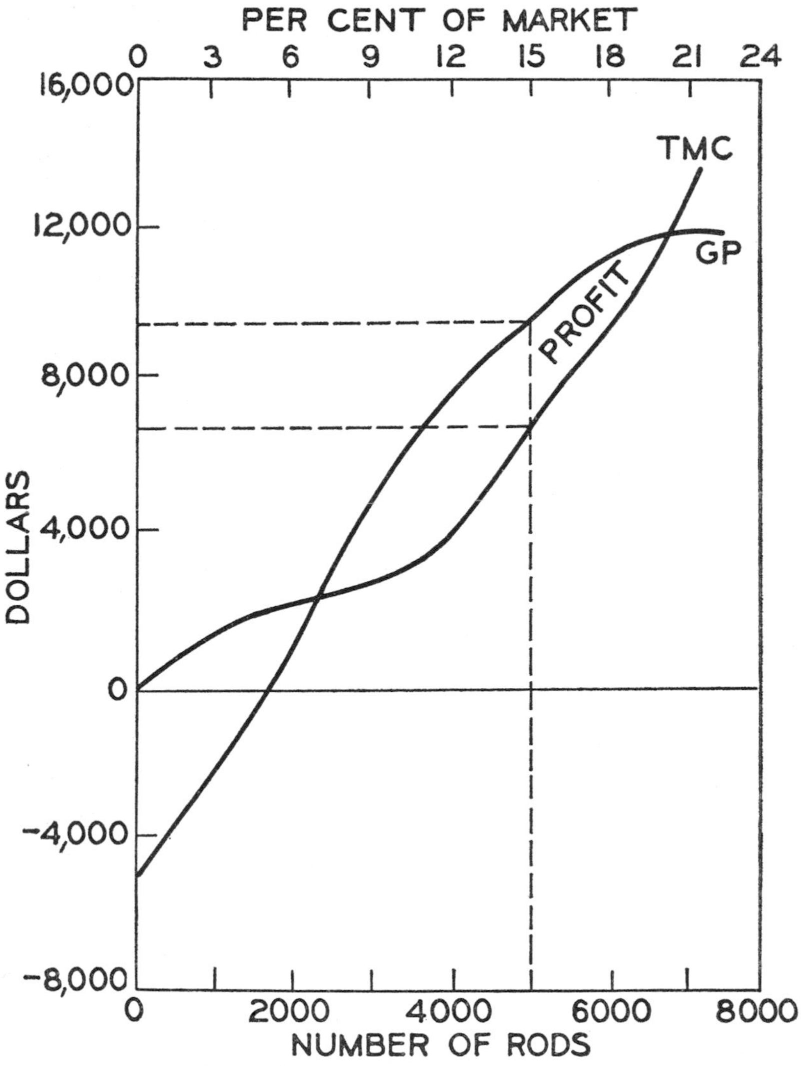

GP   = Gross Profit, Total Revenue minus Total Production
       Cost at each level of output.

TMC = Total Marketing Cost necessary to market each level
       of output (assuming a price of $3.98 and an optimum
       combination of product and sales effort).

tion, it is possible to *estimate* the optimum combinations of
product and sales effort for each price (the procedure of Stage I)
and then to select the profit or security maximizing marketing
expenditure for each price (Stage II). The diagrams for the
prices of $3.49, $3.98, and $4.49 may be drawn separately and
compared, or they may be superimposed upon one diagram as
illustrated in Figure V. If a very large number of prices were
under consideration, it would be simplest to compare individual
charts, rather than superimposing them on one diagram. Also,
if the share of market is an important consideration, separate
charts would be necessary in that the price charged by the firm
will probably affect the prices of competitors. Assuming price
elasticity, this would affect the sales volume of the industry, which
is the basis for computing the firm's share of market.[4]

In Figure V it is assumed that the maximum short-run profit
is the sole goal of the entrepreneur. Given the three relevant
prices, the various optimum marketing expenditures available to
the firm, and the resulting total revenues (sales volumes) and
minimum total costs (production and marketing), the entrepreneur may select the combination of price, product, and sales
effort that maximizes profits.

In the situation pictured in Figure V, the firm's demand is
fairly elastic. The line TR_1 shows the revenue that would result
from each volume of sales at a price of $4.49. However, to attain
sales at the increased price of $4.49, the firm would have to
increase its nonprice competitive efforts and expenditures considerably. As a result, profit would decline at all levels of sales.
The profit maximizing sales volume would remain at about
4,000 units as shown by the vertical profit line X. If price is

---

[4] The nonprice competitive strategy might also induce rival reactions and lead
to a change in the level of industry sales.

Figure V

OPTIMUM COMBINATIONS AT VARIOUS PRICES

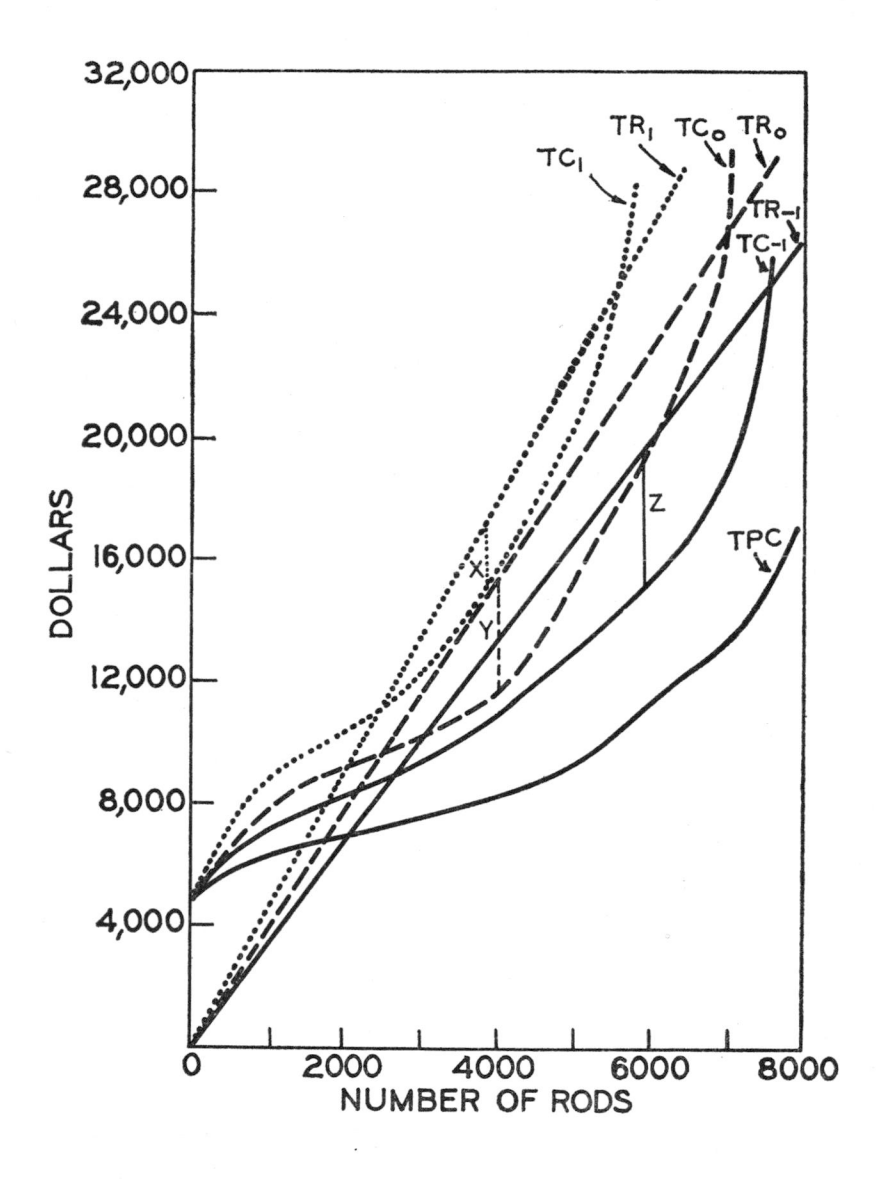

LEGEND FOR FIGURE V

TR_1 = Total Revenue resulting from each level of sales at a price of $4.49.

TC_1 = Total Cost necessary to obtain each level of sales at a price of $4.49.

X = Maximum profit attainable at a price of $4.49.

TR_0 = Total Revenue resulting from each level of sales at a price of $3.98.

TC_0 = Total Cost necessary to obtain each level of sales at a price of $3.98.

Y = Maximum profit attainable at a price of $3.98.

TR_{-1} = Total Revenue resulting from each level of sales at a price of $3.49.

TC_{-1} = Total Cost necessary to obtain each level of sales at a price of $3.49.

Z = Maximum profit attainable at a price of $3.49.

TPC = Total Production Cost for each level of sales.

decreased to $3.49 per fishing rod, nonprice competitive expenditures may be substantially reduced. The line TR_{-1} shows the revenue that would result from each sales volume, and the curve TC_{-1} shows the total estimated production and marketing costs necessary to obtain each sales volume. The maximum profit combination for the price of $3.49 is shown by the vertical profit line Z. At this point, 6,000 fishing rods would be sold. Production costs would be $11,000, and it is estimated that $4,500 of nonprice competitive efforts would be necessary to sell 6,000 rods. The total revenue would be 6,000 times $3.49 or $20,940. An estimated profit of $5,440 would result ($20,940 Total Revenue less $15,500 Total Costs = $5,440). This particular combination of price, production, and marketing costs represents the estimated profit maximizing combination for the firm.

If security is an objective, and its manifestation is a resistance to price change, the firm need only consider cost and revenue curves TC_0 and TR_0. If security is sought through following the prices of a price leader, and the price leader has established a new price of $4.49, only the curves TC_1 and TR_1 need be considered. If holding or attaining a certain share of the market is the firm's criterion for security, then the marketing cost and

revenue combinations for each price should be drawn separately as previously shown in Figure IV. Once the coveted share of the market is specified, the firm may select the combination of price and marketing expenditures that is expected to yield the maximum profits at the coveted share of the market.

Conclusion

The two-stage approach outlined above would be unworkable if prices were continuous, rather than discrete. However, the assumption of a relevant range of discrete prices is realistic, and the approach has a number of advantages over traditional marginal analysis.

1. No restrictions are placed upon the shape of production cost curves. To obtain the profit maximizing solution, U-shaped production cost curves are not necessary.

2. The role of the product *and* sales efforts is incorporated into the analysis and is realistically emphasized.

3. The security motive, in terms of a sought-for share of the market or a resistance to price change, may be handled within the framework for selecting the optimum marketing strategy.

4. The approach utilizes total costs which are easier to visualize and compute than marginal costs.

The major limitation of the approach stems from economic uncertainty and the interdependence that exists among business rivals—the difficulty of forecasting the combinations of product and sales effort that will yield various levels of sales at the lowest costs of marketing. However, marketing management can *estimate* a number of combinations of product and sales efforts that will yield various levels of sales. Just as setting the price is, in practice, the selection from a few feasible prices, there is a range of discrete combinations of product and sales efforts that is feasible for the firm to consider. In other words, it is not advisable for the firm to attempt to evaluate a huge number of combinations. In fact, the *greatest* difficulty management faces

[148]

is not the *number* of combinations of price, product, and sales effort available, but the estimation of the *effects* of each combination in terms of sales, costs, and market shares.

The hypotheses relating to the importance of product effort and sales effort offer management a guide for judging the potential effects of various combinations. The two-stage approach provides a framework for pulling together price, product, sales effort, production costs, and sales revenue for estimating the optimum combination for the firm. However, it is only a theoretical guide and framework for analysis and decision making. The necessary estimates to arrive at the final decision must come from objective data and the seasoned judgment of the entrepreneur.

APPENDIX II

THE RESEARCH INSTRUMENT

MARKETING MANAGEMENT STUDY—
UNIVERSITY OF WISCONSIN

Different products sometimes require completely different marketing strategies. So that this study may be as specific as possible, please choose one particular product (or a closely related line of products) for which your marketing policies and activities are similar. In making your selection, please choose a product which is important in terms of its contribution to total sales volume or to profits. Please indicate your product choice below.

Specific Product or Product Line ....

Some products sell in more than one market, and each market may require a separate marketing strategy. For instance, automobile batteries are sold directly to manufacturers for original equipment purposes and to the public for replacement purposes. These two markets require different marketing strategies. Please select a *major* market *for the product chosen above* and indicate that market below.

Selected Market ....

Characteristics Of Your Product And Its Market

In this section you are asked to estimate certain factors con-

cerning the product and market selected above. In the following questions, *the term "consumer" refers to the person or company who uses your product in the form that it leaves your factory.* For example, the consumer of a home mixer would be the housewife, the consumer of a raw material would be the next processor, and the consumer of a service would be the person or company for whom the service is performed.

Please circle the number which best approximates the nature of the product and market that you selected.

Level of Comprehension. What is the level of comprehension and knowledge that the consumer has in regard to your product, and particularly its want-satisfying power? This would include the consumer's comprehension of the product's composition, functioning, application, and its ability to satisfy wants and needs.

1	2	3	4	5
High Comprehension and Knowledge		Moderate Comprehension and Knowledge		Low Comprehension and Knowledge

Product Complexity. How complex is the product? For example, paper for wrapping packages usually would not be considered a technical product. However, paper for insulation in electric transformers would be considered technical in nature.

1	2	3	4	5
Highly Technical		Semi- Technical		Non- Technical

Value of Typical Purchase. What is the value of the typical purchase *by the consumer?* The value of the typical purchase is found by multiplying the average price of the product times the typical quantity bought by the consumer per transaction or sale.

Estimated Typical Purchase $...

[151]

Buyer Effort. What is the effort of the buyer—the amount of time, expense, and consideration which the typical consumer puts forth in purchasing the product? This category would include searching for alternative sources of supply, seeking specific brands, obtaining price information, and evaluating technical aspects of the product in relation to the use to which the product will be put.

1	2	3	4	5
Great Effort		Moderate Effort		Little or No Effort

Buying Motives. What are the consumer's motives for buying the product? The two extreme types of buying motives are those which are *operational* and those which are *socio-psychological. Operational* buying motives include those reasons for purchase which are directly related to the anticipated physical performance of the product, such as productivity, durability, efficiency, and profitability. *Socio-psychological* buying motives comprise those reasons for the purchase which are only indirectly related to the anticipated performance of the product, but are directly related to the consumer's social and psychological interpretation of the product. Examples of socio-psychological buying motives are the customer's image of the product in terms of prestige, social popularity, sexual appeal, youthfulness, recreation, and fashion.

1	2	3	4	5
Operational Buying Motives		Equally Strong Operational and Socio-Psychological Buying Motives		Socio-Psychological Buying Motives

Characteristics Of Your Marketing Program

In this section of the study, please estimate the relative importance of the basic elements of the marketing strategy for the product and market you have selected. In each question you are given 100 points to allocate among the elements of your marketing strategy. *Please use your judgment to allocate these 100*

points to the elements in relation to their contribution to the success of the product in the specific market that you have selected.

I. PRODUCT EFFORTS include product planning, product research and development, product testing and the services accompanying the product. Considering your specific PRODUCT EFFORTS, please allocate 100 points among the following subordinate areas according to their contribution to the total product program.

.... *Market research* relating to product planning and development, and product testing.

.... *Technical research, development, and laboratory testing* of new products and improvements of existing products.

.... *Product research* relating to the development of *product styling* and fashions.

.... *Presale service* such as product application engineering.

.... *Postsale service* such as product installation, maintenance, and guarantee service.

.... Other (please specify)
_____
100 Points

II. SALES EFFORTS include such areas as sales management, personal selling, advertising, promotional programs, and all other forms of marketing communications. With regard to the SALES EFFORTS for your selected product and market, please allocate 100 points among the following facets of this major policy area according to their relative importance.

.... *Product branding and promotional packaging.*

.... *Printed media advertising* in newspapers, magazines, and brochures.

.... *Broadcast media advertising* on radio and television.

.... *Sales management and personal selling* including all

sales management activities (e.g., training, supervision, etc.) and the sales efforts of your company management personnel.

.... *Special promotional activities* such as promotional warranties, trade shows, dealer aids, and product displays.

.... Other (please specify)
_____
100 Points

III. DISTRIBUTION includes the selection, coordination, and evaluation of channels, transportation, warehousing and inventory control. Please allocate 100 points among the following facets of DISTRIBUTION according to their relative importance.

.... *Transportation.*

.... *Warehousing and inventory control.*

.... *Determination of the basic channels* of distribution to be utilized.

.... *Selection of individual establishments within the basic channels.*

.... *Manufacturer's efforts to develop and assist the channel of distribution.*

.... Other (please specify)
_____
100 Points

IV. PRICING STRATEGY includes price determination, pricing policies, and specific pricing strategies over which you exercise some degree of control. Please allocate 100 points among the following possible facets of PRICING STRATEGY according to their importance in your marketing program.

.... *Cost-plus-desired profit* or standard cost pricing.

.... *Pricing according to competitive levels*—pricing at the prevailing competitive price.

.... *Pricing at a certain percent above or below competitors' prices.*

.... *Pricing according to what the market will bear*—price based on estimated value of the product to the consumer.

.... *Pricing based on governmental rules and regulations.*

.... Other (please specify)

_____
100 Points

V. Please allocate 100 points among the following four major policy areas according to their relative importance in your *marketing strategy*.

.... *Product Efforts* — includes product planning, product R & D, product testing and the services accompanying the product.

.... *Sales Efforts* — includes sales management and personal selling, advertising, promotional programs, and all other marketing communications.

.... *Distribution* — includes the selection, coordination, and evaluation of channels, transportation, and inventory control.

.... *Pricing Strategy* — includes price determination, pricing policies, and specific strategies over which you exercise some degree of control.

.... Other (please specify)

_____
100 Points

Classification Information

To aid in the interpretation of the data you have given, would you please complete the following questions? *All information will be completely confidential* and will be used only to classify your earlier responses into general categories for analysis.

1. Name and address of person completing this questionnaire (optional, but will be needed if you would like a complimentary copy of the research report).

[155]

....

....

....

2. Title of person completing this questionnaire.

....

3. Please check the range which approximates the sales volume *of the product, or product line,* during the last fiscal year.

.... Less than $500,000 .... $1,000,000 to $10,000,000

.... $500,000 to $1,000,000 .... $10,000,000 or more

4. What is your approximate share of the market *for this product or product line* in the market you specified? (If you don't know the share, please estimate.)

.... less than 5% .... 25% to 35%

.... 5% to 15% .... 35% to 45%

.... 15% to 25% .... 45% or more

5. Would you please estimate what percent of your *total cost* for this product is *marketing cost?*

.... Less than 5% .... 20% to 25%

.... 5% to 10% .... 25% to 30%

.... 10% to 15% .... 30% or more

.... 15% to 20%

THANK YOU FOR YOUR COOPERATION!
IT IS VERY MUCH APPRECIATED.

BIBLIOGRAPHY

American Economic Association. *Readings in Price Theory.* Homewood, Illinois: Richard D. Irwin, Inc., 1952.

Backman, Jules. *Advertising and Competition.* New York: New York University Press, 1967.

Bain, Joe S. *Barriers to New Competition.* Cambridge: Harvard University Press, 1956.

Bain, Joe S. *Pricing, Distribution, and Employment.* New York: Henry Holt and Company, 1958.

Baumol, W. S. "On the Role of Marketing Theory." *Journal of Marketing,* XXI (April, 1957), 413.

Bertrand, Joseph. Review of Cournot, "Recherches." *Journal des Savants.* Paris: 1883.

Buzzell, R. D. "Is Marketing a Science?" *Harvard Business Review,* XLI (January, 1963), 32-40.

Chamberlin, Edward H. *The Theory of Monopolistic Competition.* 7th ed. Cambridge: Harvard University Press, 1958.

Cournot, Antoine. *Recherches sur les Principes Mathematiques de la Theorie des Richesses.* Translated by Nathaniel T. Baion. ("Researches into the Mathematical Principles of the Theory of Wealth.") Paris: 1838.

Edgeworth, F. Y. "La Teoria Pura del Monopolio." *Gionale degli Economists,* XV, (1897). A translation into English appears in his *Papers Relating to Political Economy,* Vol. I. London: Macmillan and Company, 1925.

Fellner, William. *Competition Among the Few.* New York: Augustus M. Kelly, 1960.

Hall, R. L., and Hitch, C. J. "Price Theory and Business Behavior," *Oxford Studies in the Price Mechanism.* Oxford: Clarendon Press, Oxford University, 1951.

New York Times. "Advertising: A Reassuring Antitrust Word," February 9, 1967.

Robinson, Joan. *The Economics of Imperfect Competition.* London: Macmillan and Company, 1934.

Romney, George. "The Compact Car Revolution—A Case History in Consumerism." *Michigan Business Review,* II (July, 1959), 1-7.

Rostow, Walt W. "The Concept of a National Market and Its Economic Growth Implications." *Proceedings of the American Marketing Association,* (Fall, 1965), 19.

Say, Jean Baptiste. *A Treatise on Political Economy.* Paris: 1803.

Smith, Adam. *The Wealth of Nations.* New York: Random House, Inc., 1937.

Stigler, George J. "The Kinky Oligopoly Demand Curve and Rigid Prices." *Journal of Political Economy,* LV (1947), 432-449.

Stigler, George J. *Theory of Price.* New York: The Macmillan Company, 1946.

Stonier, Alfred W., and Hague, Douglas C. *A Textbook of Economic Theory.* New York: Longmans Green and Co., 1956.

Sweezy, Paul M. "Demand Under Conditions of Oligopoly." *Journal of Political Economy,* XLVII (1939), 568-573.

Udell, Jon G., and LeGrande, Bruce. "Consumer Behavior in the Market Place: An Empirical Study of Television and Furniture Purchasing with Theoretical Implications." *Journal of Retailing,* 40 (Fall, 1964), 32-40.

Udell, Jon G. *A Model of Non-Price Competitive Strategy.* Madison, Wisconsin: Bureau of Business Research and Service, School of Business, University of Wisconsin, 1963.

Udell, Jon G. "A New Approach to Consumer Motivation." *Journal of Retailing,* XL (Winter, 1964-65), 6-10.

Udell, Jon G. "Prepurchase Behavior of Buyers of Small Electrical Appliances." *Journal of Marketing,* XXX (October, 1966), 50-52.

U. S. Department of Commerce. *Statistical Abstract of the United States.* Washington, D. C.: Government Printing Office, 1969.

Wall Street Journal. "Firms Strive to Avoid Introducing Products that Nobody Will Buy." March 6, 1967.

Westing, J. H., Fine, I. V., and Zenz, Gary J. *Purchasing Management.* 3rd ed. New York: John Wiley and Sons, Inc., 1969.

Wisconsin State Journal. "FTC Report Critical of Gasoline Gimmicks." June 30, 1967.

DATE DUE

MAY 20.1980			
MAY 19 80			
NOV. 13.1980			
JAN. 15.1981			
AUG. 20.1981			
SEP. 2 2 '8			
SEP. 27.1982			
MAR. 12.1984			
AUG. 5 1990			
AUG. 12.1998			
GAYLORD			PRINTED IN U.S.A.